STAR SIGNS

AN ASTROLOGICAL GUIDE
FOR YOU AND YOUR PET

JOHN G. SUTTON

ELEMENT CHILDREN'S BOOKS

SHAFTESBURY, DORSET · BOSTON, MASSACHUSETTS · MELBOURNE, VICTORIA

*This book is dedicated to my dear wife Mary Sutton.
Without this lady's help and support there would be
no book, no future and probably no John G. Sutton.*

ACKNOWLEDGEMENT

The author wishes to acknowledge the assistance and
technical expertise of the psychic astrologer Mr.
Gary Dakin of Manchester, England. Gary proved to be
a mine of detailed information and without his
assistance many of the long-range predictions could
not have been made.

© Element Children's Books 1998

First published in Great Britain in 1998 by
Element Children's Books Shaftesbury, Dorset SP7 8BP

Published and distributed in the USA in 1998 by Element Books Inc.
160 North Washington Street, Boston MA02114

Published in Australia in 1998 by Element Books Limited
and distributed by Penguin Books Australia Ltd,
487 Maroondah Highway, Ringwood, Victoria 3134

Copyright © 1998 Text John G. Sutton
The moral rights of the author and illustrator have been asserted.

British Library Cataloguing in Publication data available.
Library of Congress Cataloguing in Publication data available.

ISBN 1 90188 1806

Cover design by Mandy Sherliker
Printed and bound in China

CONTENTS

ASTRO-DOWSING CHART

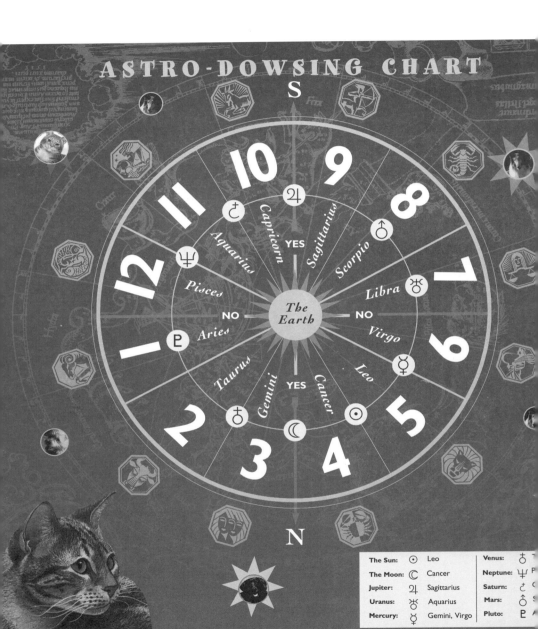

S

10 9 8 11 7 12 6 1 5 2 4 3

YES

NO — The Earth — NO

YES

Capricorn
Aquarius
Sagittarius
Pisces
Scorpio
Libra
Aries
Virgo
Taurus
Leo
Gemini
Cancer

N

The Sun:	☉	Leo	Venus:	♀	
The Moon:	☽	Cancer	Neptune:	♆	P
Jupiter:	♃	Sagittarius	Saturn:	♄	
Uranus:	♅	Aquarius	Mars:	♂	S
Mercury:	☿	Gemini, Virgo	Pluto:	♇	A

INTRODUCTION

From the ancient civilization of Babylonia came the belief that our future can be mapped out by reference to the stars. Look up into the heavens on a clear and cloudless night! There you will see proud Leo the Lion prowling through the sky with Taurus the Bull and Cancer the Crab, but what does it all mean?

Thousands of years ago the wise ones charted the stars in the firmament and concluded that people born on certain days of the year, under certain stars, had the same kind of characters as others born at the same time. Over the centuries they developed a system of predicting a person's future by making a chart of the stars which they grouped into twelve signs that form the zodiac. Using this, the wise ones could then cast a horoscope by recording which planets were in which sign at the time of a person's birth, and how they related to one another. This system is the basis of Western astrology. Today's popular star-sign columns use only the position of the Sun.

Here is an introduction to the many mysteries that surround astrology. The sections cover many of the main aspects of this subject, from star-sign characteristics to numerology. There is also a unique and totally new system called astro-dowsing. This enables you easily to cast a horoscope for yourself and your pet, without mathematical calculations and tables.

As the age of Aquarius dawns, the era of enlightenment is here, so tune in, and turn over the pages. There are more things in the universe than can be explained by conventional science — why Superman wears his underpants outside his trousers is one, astrology is another.

> Twinkle, twinkle, little star!
> How I wonder what sign you are!
> I am Leo, bold and crazy,
> Would write more but I'm too lazy.

Please do enjoy reading and thinking about this, and always

remember, you are an individual, totally unique and unlike any other human being on Earth, thank goodness!

Best wishes,

John G. Sutton

JOHN G. SUTTON

YOUR OWN
AND YOUR
PET'S STAR SIGNS

This section introduces you to the signs of the zodiac and offers an insight into the main characteristics of human beings and animals born under them. To begin with you must establish within which sign you and your pet were born. All you need to do is find the dates of birth for you and your pet in the list of star signs below.

SIGNS OF THE ZODIAC

ARIES..21 MARCH—19 APRIL

TAURUS...20 APRIL—20 MAY

GEMINI...21 MAY—20 JUNE

CANCER...21 JUNE—22 JULY

LEO..23 JULY—22 AUGUST

VIRGO.........................23 AUGUST—22 SEPTEMBER

LIBRA..........................23 SEPTEMBER—23 OCTOBER

SCORPIO.....................24 OCTOBER—22 NOVEMBER

SAGITTARIUS..............23NOVEMBER—21 DECEMBER

CAPRICORN.................22 DECEMBER—20 JANUARY

AQUARIUS....................21 JANUARY—18 FEBRUARY

PISCES.............................19 FEBRUARY—20 MARCH

My date of birth is:...

My star sign is:..

My pet's date of birth is:...

My pet's star sign is:...

If you don't know the date of birth of your pet, take the Star-Sign Assessment Test (page 43) to find out the likeliest sign. The section on astro-dowsing may also help you to decide your pet's star sign. Once you have determined this, you can go on to read about the characteristics of your pet's sign as well as your own.

ARIES THE RAM

ELEMENT: fire
RULERS: Mars and Pluto
COLORS: red, pink
STONES: garnet, ruby, bloodstone

YOU

POSITIVE CHARACTERISTICS

STRONG WILLPOWER

There is no doubt in your mind that you can do things. When you decide to undertake any task, you see it through with grim determination. Often you will seem to be obstinate, because you just will not give in. Once you start a job, you finish it at all costs. Sometimes people think you go too far, but woe betide anyone brave or foolish enough to tell you that you are banging your head against a brick wall. The Aries boy will pursue the girl of his dreams without any hesitation and will usually win her in the end. The Aries girl will use all sorts of clever tricks to capture her ideal lover.

HIGH ACHIEVER

Your ability to succeed is due in no small way to your determination, but you are also a very organized person. You like everything to be in place; if it isn't, you get rather angry. You are ambitious and aim for the top of any career that you choose. Many great writers are born under the sign of Aries: their ability to apply themselves single-mindedly to writing brings success. Arians also make very powerful leaders, because they believe so strongly in themselves that others follow. Once in command, the Aries leader is a force to be reckoned with; there is no stopping them. Top careers involve independent action: entrepreneur, company director, lawyer, record producer.

NEGATIVE CHARACTERISTICS

STUBBORN

Your self-belief often gets the better of you in relationships. You simply can't believe that your friends don't share your enthusiasm for projects. Often you will expect people to do things that interest you and can't understand that they don't interest them. This is because you're so single-minded.

You tend to be very impatient and want everything done right now, not tomorrow. You can also be very critical: if someone does something that isn't absolutely as you would like it, then you just tell them. This can cause offence, since most people do not like being told they are wrong.

HEALTH

Aries people are very hard-working and need more rest than most. They tend to use their brains and place themselves under a lot of pressure. A typical Arian will often suffer from headaches, owing to continuous concentration. Aries-sign people are prone to accidents that injure their heads, causing cuts and bruises. Many have problems with acne on their faces.

On the plus side, Arian people have very strong hearts and good appetites; they just love food.

YOUR PET

POSITIVE CHARACTERISTICS

SELF-DETERMINED

Dogs born under the sign of Aries are so determined to do what they want that training them is always difficult. Arian dogs are definitely fun — if you like very long walks. Arian cats are so certain of themselves that you will soon accept that they know best. It matters not to these proud creatures what you think: eventually they will have their way, and that's that. A typical Aries pet is very stubborn.

MAGICAL FUN CREATURE

Aries pets will win your heart in one magic moment of fun. Somehow they seem able to sense your feelings and know when you want to play, even if you don't show it. There is no point trying to ignore Aries pets; they will continue attempting to play with you until you give in.

Typical Aries cats will purr with pleasure when they achieve their goal of gaining your undivided attention. Arian dogs will bark the house down if you even think about ignoring them. Pets born under the sign of Aries get what they want and that usually means you.

NEGATIVE CHARACTERISTICS

SELF-CENTRED

A typical Aries pet will only do exactly what it wants to do. There seems to be no way you can persuade these pets to accept your instructions. Once an Arian cat has made up its mind to sleep snuggled up on your favourite chair, it will take some shifting. An Aries dog will often form a real bond of love with just one person and ignore everyone else. All Aries pets tend to be self-centered. There is not much point in trying to change them, so justaccept them as they are.

HEALTH

The Aries pet is often accident-prone and likes to live dangerously. Being stubborn, these pets think cars should stop for them. Falling off things is a typical Aries pet trick; cats are especially likely to do this. An Arian dog will not think twice before it dives into a river. Fighting with other dogs is also typical. Aries dogs have such a high opinion of themselves that any challenge by another dog is met with an immediate response.

All Aries pets like a lot to eat. They live fast lives and need the extra nourishment.

PET TIPS

If you own an Aries pet, you are in for some fun, even if it might not always seem so at the time. When in doubt, slip your Aries pet a titbit for a treat — they are always ready to eat. Train them early, because once they get set in their ways, you have no chance.

TAURUS THE BULL

ELEMENT: earth
RULER: Venus
COLORS: blue, violet, purple (avoid red!)
STONES: emerald, turquoise, lapis lazuli

YOU

POSITIVE CHARACTERISTICS

POWERFUL PERSONALITY

Born under the sign of Taurus, you are blessed with an almost magnetic personality. Others seem drawn to you and your hypnotic eyes. The power you have to attract people makes you determined always to look your best. A typical Taurean will have lots of fine clothes and all the best designer labels. No other sign is as conscious as you are of their appearance. With all the attention you get comes responsibility - others often look to you to lead them. Yours is a very strong sign, so be aware of your authority.

The Taurus boy will fall in love quickly and dazzle the girl of his choice with his sense of style. The Taurus girl will attract all the boys with her good looks and lovely clothes.

SUCCESS WITH MATERIAL THINGS

As an earth sign you love to control material property, and Taureans particularly enjoy owning all kinds of consumer goods, toys and gadgets, and all the latest fashions. Once you make your mind up to have something, you won't stop until you get it. A beautiful home is also important to a Taurean.

Your natural leadership qualities enable you to rise to the very top in any chosen career. Those born under the sign of Taurus are also very artistic. Many Taureans have a poetic nature and they are often musical. Some great writers and artists are born under this sign. They are seldom overlooked: if a Taurean decides to write a poem, they will do so to the best of their ability and insist that everyone else listen while they read it.

Top careers for Taureans include creative management, fashion designer, author, architect.

NEGATIVE CHARACTERISTICS

PROUD

Being born under a proud sign, Taureans will not accept that there are limits to their abilities, and this can bring trouble. A very demanding and determined sign, Taurus quite often runs at life like a bull in a china shop. Sometimes Taureans will go too far to please those they want to impress.

Taureans are more upset than other signs by discomfort and hardship.

Often those born under the sign of Taurus will expect far too much from those they profess to love. This can create stress and many Taureans have lots of relationships before they find their one true love, if they ever do. Expect plenty of break-ups before the Taurean settles down.

HEALTH

Your general health is excellent. Taureans are robust and often very strong, with muscular bodies and big hearts. The only problem area is the throat and sometimes the lungs — no smoking for this sign!

YOUR PET

POSITIVE CHARACTERISTICS

LOYAL AND HOME-LOVING

A typical Taurean pet will know whom it trusts and loves. Once this is established, it will be your friend for life. Pets born under the sign of Taurus will be dependable, but they need stability and lots of love.

Taurean pets just love their home. They are at their best within the boundary of the house or area they recognize as theirs, and won't stray far.

DETERMINED GUARD

The Taurean dog is as easy-going a creature as you could wish to meet, unless someone or something threatens its home. They make good guard dogs because they are so fond of their own particular space and possessions. They love to have lots of little playthings around them.

A Taurean cat just purrs with pleasure in its home, but won't like being disturbed. Take it away from a familiar place and it'll growl like a tiger.

NEGATIVE CHARACTERISTICS

OBSTINATE

Strangers beware of the Taurus dog! They like those they know, and the rest can go run. Taurean cats are exceptionally lazy. They will cuddle up in a contented ball and ignore everything except food.

If Taurus pets ever lose one of their favorite possessions, they won't rest until they've found it. Watch out for your Taurus dog digging up your yard in search of a lost bone.

The typical Taurus pet can be so obstinate that training it can be a problem. Start training as early as you can with a Taurus pet. Once it has mastered something, it will never forget. This trait can have its drawbacks, especially if your Taurus dog has learned to destroy the morning newspaper and eat the mail.

HEALTH

Some Taurus pets can seem withdrawn, but just give them lots of love and plenty of home comforts. They are unusually strong for their breed and don't like being picked on, so get ready to patch these warrior pets up.

PET TIPS

At home, cared for and loved, the Taurus pet is all you could want. But they hate being in strange surroundings.   And the typical Taurus dog needs lots of exercise.

GEMINI THE TWINS

ELEMENT: air
RULER: Mercury
COLORS: silver, glistening white, metallic gray
STONES: sapphire, diamond, all glittering stones

YOU

POSITIVE CHARACTERISTICS

CLEVER AND FULL OF FUN

As a Gemini you are naturally very clever and quick to learn. You use your knowledge as a kind of tickling stick to make others laugh. Your idea of a good joke often involves an odd approach to situations.

Others find you either very funny or a pain. Your ability to outwit your rivals in an argument gives you a real advantage which, if used wisely, can bring success. There is no other star sign quite like Gemini — victims of your wit will no doubt be very thankful for this.

WONDERFUL COMMUNICATOR

A true Gemini can charm the monkeys out of the trees. They are smooth talkers, delightful company, and always entertaining. The Gemini boy will have many girl friends and convince each of them that she is his only true love. At the time even he may believe this to be so. The Gemini girl has the most wonderful way with words. She can talk her way out of almost any difficult situation, and with these flirty types there are going to be plenty of those.

This is a very busy sign. Typical Geminis will always be changing their minds, first one thing, then another. Far from boring, but often very puzzling and complex.

Top careers for Gemini usually involve communication skills: public relations, lecturer, travel agent. With some self-discipline, those born under Gemini can be brilliant actors, lawyers, or diplomats. Their ability to make others believe what they say is second to no other sign.

NEGATIVE CHARACTERISTICS

THOUGHTLESS

Because those born under Gemini are so quick, they are often far ahead of their friends and sometimes mock them for being slower. The Gemini sense of humour can be strange often very sarcastic. Although not deliberately cruel, typical Geminis will not think twice about saying hurtful things to those who love them.

HEALTH

Gemini people are inclined to suffer from chesty colds and often have trouble with their lungs. When they get a bad cough, it seems to last for ages. The real Gemini types may be nervous and high-strung and can be very sensitive to criticism.

YOUR PET

POSITIVE CHARACTERISTICS

QUICK TO LEARN

Probably the most mixed-up pets in the entire zodiac are born under the sign of Gemini. So quick are they to learn that boredom soon sets in and they move on to meet other challenges. The typical Gemini cat will rapidly use up its supposed quota of nine lives as it ventures where other signs fear to tread. If your cat likes jumping out of windows into almost empty space as it searches for adventure, then the odds are that it's a Gemini. The dog born under this sign will never rest until it has discovered everything there is to know about you and its home. Gemini pets want to roam free in order to conquer the world.

CHARMING AND LOVING

The Gemini pet is just hungry to love and be loved. But there is a catch. These charming and usually delightful pets are rather quick to switch their affections from one person to another. The Gemini dog will be all over you one minute and the next completely ignore you as it chases someone else. If Gemini cats don't get constant attention and love, they soon move on elsewhere.

Of all the signs in the zodiac, Gemini pets are the most likely to let you know if things are not exactly as they want them. Should you fail to respond to their demands, you can wave them bye-bye. Gemini pets are all Gypsies at heart.

NEGATIVE CHARACTERISTICS

FICKLE AND CHANGEABLE

Being very fickle with their love, Gemini pets can hurt their owners, who may believe that the pet is just using them as a meal ticket. Some Gemini cats are so determined to have what they want that they flit from home to home. The idea that you or anyone else can actually own a Gemini cat is a mistake. Gemini cats think they own you.

The dog born under Gemini is also very self-centred. Such pooches have more pals than you can count and will run off to play with them, given the opportunity.

Of course Gemini pets do love their owners; they just forget to let them know at times. They can also get bored very quickly and sulk.

HEALTH

Gemini pets are often touchy about the kind of food they like and can change their minds overnight. Some Gemini pets will have digestive problems and these are usually fussy eaters.

PET TIPS

Owning a Gemini pet is a challenge. If you meet its demands you will have a loving friend, until it changes its mind. Expect lots of fun with a Gemini pet, and many strange demands. If possible, don't keep it shut up indoors. Even Gemini rabbits like a walk out and you should make sure that your garden is secure, otherwise bye-bye, bunny.

 # CANCER THE CRAB

ELEMENT: water
RULER: the Moon
COLORS: green, white, cream
STONES: moonstone, opal, crystal

YOU

POSITIVE CHARACTERISTICS

GOOD HOMEMAKER

Your home is very important to you. Those born under the influence of Cancer love to have a secure and comfortable place to live. You go to extremes to make sure that your own space is just the way you want itto be. Neat and naturally tidy, the Cancer-sign girl will have a place for everything. Cancer-sign boys are unusually clean and always have their sports clothing washed and pressed, even if they have to do it themselves.

Like the crab that is the symbol of this sign, all Cancerians need to feel protected. They make wonderful, loving partners and are very loyal. When a Cancerian falls in love and gives their heart, it is forever.

HARD-WORKING AND DEDICATED

Most Cancerians are very hard-working and happiest when they are busy. They are determined to get the job done, whatever it may be, and are very dedicated to their work.

With a great imagination, the Cancer lover can create a wonderful life for the one they choose as their life's partner. Extremely sensitive to the needs of others, Cancer girls are unusually kind and generous to those they care for. The Cancer-sign boy will fall in love with one very special person and dedicate his life to her.
Cancerians are of a mystical nature and often psychic.

They often make brilliant musicians. Other top careers involve imagination and creativity: interior designer, sports-center management.

NEGATIVE CHARACTERISTICS

TOO SENSITIVE

The typical Cancer-sign person can sometimes be too sensitive to criticism. They get angry easily, and they become sad when others don't appreciate their efforts. A Cancerian will often be a rebel and some can be very difficult to get on with. This is because they have a strong psychic side to their nature and just know when things are wrong. Never try to dictate to a Cancer sign — they will bite your head off.

In love, Cancerian individuals may be overpowering. They want their partner with them all the time. If you're in love with a Cancer sign, don't cheat on them. They are gifted with a sixth sense that sets the alarm bells ringing and will react with hostility.

HEALTH

Cancerians often suffer from aches and pains in their joints. Sometimes they have trouble with their feet and need to take great care of their toes. They should also watch what they eat: shellfish and especially crabs can give them stomach troubles. Otherwise Cancerians are of general good health, with sharp eyesight and strong hands.

YOUR PET

POSITIVE CHARACTERISTICS

HOME-LOVING

Cancer-sign pets make the most home-loving friends you could wish for. They will soon snuggle down in their little bit of your house and establish a regular routine all their own. They love their own little place almost as much as they will love you for looking after them. The typical Cancer cat won't wander far from its home and rarely changes owners willingly. Cancer dogs won't let strangers near their property or their friends, so if a guard dog is what your family want, you can't do better than a big Cancer dog.

A FRIEND FOR LIFE
All pets born under the influence of Cancer are very friendly and will happily play with you all day. A Cancerian dog will often be the best friend a boy or girl could want. They will love you to bits and have the best tail wag of all the signs when they greet you. If a cuddle and a snuggle is what you want from a pet, then the Cancer cat is the one for you.

NEGATIVE CHARACTERISTICS

LAZY LUMP
Lazy lumps are typical Cancer pets, they like snoozing. The Cancer-sign dog could probably win the Olympic Gold Medal for snoring. Cats born under Cancer have a need for almost constant attention and will frequently jump up for a cuddle when you are busy trying to do something else. If you tell your Cancer sign pet off for some misdeed, it will sulk for ages. These pets are also very stubborn at times and if you try to get them to do something they don't want, well, they won't do it. Do not upset a Cancer-sign pet. They don't like arguments and can sense when you are angry. This sign has psychic powers — maybe your pet can read your mind, so think positive, loving thoughts when it's around.

HEALTH
The Cancer pet is a born worrier. They're so sensitive that they sometimes react to stress or trouble by not eating properly. Fussy with their food but, with care, no problems.

PET TIPS
Once your Cancer pet has made itself comfortable in your home, do not try to move it.

Pets born under this sign need to be given bucketfuls of love. Whenever you greet your pet, hug it, stroke it, cuddle it, and tell it you love it. Do this and you will have a friend for life.

LEO THE LION

ELEMENT: fire
RULER: the Sun
COLORS: orange, yellow, white
STONES: ruby, amber, topaz

YOU

POSITIVE CHARACTERISTICS

DYNAMIC AND DETERMINED

As a Leo you have the determination to succeed against all odds. Nothing can stop you, even defeat will pass unnoticed as you thunder on your way forward. Others see you as either a brilliant and forceful leader or as a big-head. You care intensely what your friends think about you but, more than this, you care what you think about yourself. Leos will never allow themselves to do anything less than their very best, no matter what the task.

Your fiery personality can light up any conversation and you know it. No one controls a Leo and this can get them into lots of trouble. Always ready to defend their position, real Leos would never deliberately hurt anyone, though they are so dynamic, strong, and often very charming that few can stand in their way.

FEARLESS

All true Leos know that they can't be defeated, at least in their own minds. This gives them the fearlessness they will need to tackle the almost impossible tasks they set for themselves. Being brave, the Leo boy can often get into arguments with others much, much bigger than himself.

Generous in victory and incapable of believing itself beaten, Leo is the warrior sign of the zodiac.

Dynamic leaders, Leos make good politicians, military officers, and show-business promoters.

NEGATIVE CHARACTERISTICS

CRITICAL AND AGGRESSIVE

Leos expect so much of themselves that anything that seems like failure hurts them. Having been told that they're out of order, Leos can be aggressive.

Being so sure of themselves, Leos have great difficulty in accepting that they may be wrong. Some Leos become very angry with others who do not share their point of view. This characteristic can create a lot of trouble in the schoolyard.

HEALTH

Leos quite often suffer from heart problems. They put so much effort into their lives that the strain is bound to tell somewhere. Sometimes Leos get headaches. These are usually brought on by overwork: once started, Leos just don't know when to stop.

YOUR PET

POSITIVE CHARACTERISTICS

ATTITUDE PLUS

Like the lion that is the symbol of this sign, Leo pets are the aristocrats of the animal kingdom. They instinctively know that they are in charge and strut round like the royalty they think they are. A typical Leo dog will have a real attitude and assumes that everyone is looking at it. The Leo cat can be very vain and is forever cleaning and smoothing its fur. Leos are the show-business stars of pets, always posing and preening. No other sign is as aware of its own importance. Heap praise upon Leo pets, tell them they look great, and they will light up your life with their magnificent personalities.

BRAVE AND LOYAL

A Leo dog will often get into fights with other dogs, no matter how much bigger they are. Leo cats also are battlers, and no matter how often they get hurt, they always go back for more. Any Leo pet you may own will be a handful. They are just so full of themselves. As guards, the Leo dogs would stop an elephant or an armed burglar — better not cross this dog's path!

Leo pets are very loyal, and are at their best when being showered with love and attention.

NEGATIVE CHARACTERISTICS

A SHOW-OFF

Leo pets can create big trouble in any home when they think they're being ignored. The Leo dog will growl and roar like a lion and often destroys furniture and anything else it can get its teeth into. The Leo cat will get under your feet or on top of your desk and roll about, making a great fuss. Leo pets are always seeking attention. There's only one thing you can do: give in and love them.

HEALTH

Fighting with everything that moves makes Leo pets vulnerable to injury. They get cut, bitten, scratched, and chewed, but don't seem to notice or care. A Leo pet would rather have a fight than a bowl of its favorite food. They know no fear and often live short but highly dramatic and interesting lives.

PET TIPS

You must let your Leo pet know who is in charge from the very first day it enters your home. But never ignore it. Give this pet lots of attention, stroke it, talk to it, praise it, love it. Then your Leo pet will glow with pride and be the best friend you could ever want.

These pets are great fun, but as they are very strong, be careful when playing with them — they like to win.

 # VIRGO THE VIRGIN

ELEMENT: earth
RULER: Mercury
COLORS: pale pastel shades, silver
STONES: diamond, pearl, emerald

YOU

POSITIVE CHARACTERISTICS

BRILLIANT BRAINS

Born under the influence of Virgo, you will be very clever and have an ability to store lots of facts in your brain. Your understanding of quite difficult problems makes you one of the smartest kids on the block.

Others admire your quick thinking.

No one pulls the wool over your eyes. You can spot an error miles away and have no hesitation in pointing it out. You will be the one others ask to organize functions, raffles, club outings, and other events.

FASTIDIOUS

Often strikingly attractive, Virgo-sign people have a virtuous air about them that makes others want them as their best friends. As young people, Virgos tend to be pure in thought and deed. Their personal appearance is always neat, clean, and tidy. They are a real example and others respect this.

In love, the Virgo boy seeks the perfect partner and, because he is so quick-witted, often wins her. The Virgo girl is always looking for Mr Right and will only accept what she sees as the best-looking boy in town.

Many born under the sign of Virgo lead very successful lives and rise to the top of quite challenging professions. Your organizational skills with facts and people offer you a lot of chances in life. Top Virgo careers include lawyer, doctor, accountant, business manager, employment agent, publisher, and editor.

NEGATIVE CHARACTERISTICS
FUSSY FAULT-FINDER
As a Virgo you can see exactly what's wrong with most things. You don't like anything out of place and will act to correct it, given the chance. If others fall below the very high standard you set, then you just tell them. This can cause some to think you are being too fussy. You can't help finding faults; to you they stick out like a sore thumb. As a Virgo you hate mess, dislike untidiness, and have probably been known to brush the dandruff off your friends' shoulders. Virgos think this kind of behaviour is called for, so don't worry, it's the way you are.

HEALTH
Virgo is probably the healthiest of all the star signs. Virgos tend to imagine they're ill when in fact they are in good health. Every little twinge is a major worry to typical Virgos. Main problem areas are the chest and lungs, but nervous disorders are definitely at the top of any Virgo ill-health list.

YOUR PET

POSITIVE CHARACTERISTICS

QUICK LEARNER

Virgo pets are quick learners and need almost no training at all. Show your Virgo dog where its lead is and it won't forget. The Virgo cat is also very smart and can find your chicken dinner even in a closed fridge.

Virgo pets are happiest in a neat and tidy space that they can make their own. They're usually very clean pets and like their bedding to be regularly washed. Never give them food in a dirty bowl.

Your Virgo pet will be watching you and, because they are so clever, will adapt to your lifestyle.

GOOD WORKER

Because they're so easy to train, Virgo dogs make wonderful workers. Many outstanding guide dogs are born under this sign. A Virgo cat will quickly outsmart all the other pets and in no time at all will have the very best bed space in the house — yours if you're not careful!

Virgo pets usually form a close bond with only one person and are extremely loyal. Owners of Virgo pets are very lucky, because these characters will give them lots and lots of love.

NEGATIVE CHARACTERISTICS

EASILY UPSET

Sometimes Virgo pets can be a little moody. They have a routine to their lives and if this is disturbed in any way, they sulk. Often Virgo dogs and cats will be very fussy eaters. If you try to change their pet food, they'll refuse it. Virgo pets like to be fed at the same time every day, and if you're late, they will remind you. If you move their basket or cushion, Virgo pets can become withdrawn. They like order and such things upset them.

HEALTH

Stress of any kind will upset a Virgo pet. House moves or just changing a well-established routine can cause the Virgo pet to worry. Once in a stressful situation, the Virgo pet will often display signs of nervous disorder, refusing food, being sick. Keep it calm, give it lots of cuddles and, if you are concerned, take it to your vet.

PET TIPS

As soon as you get a Virgo pet, do your best to let it know you're its friend. They just love being with their owner and will follow you around, given the chance. Keep their daily routine as regular as you possibly can and try to feed and walk them at the same time each day. With a nice clean bed space, lots of cuddles, and plenty of good food, your Virgo pet will be a loyal and loving a companion. Always talk to your Virgo pet — these are really clever creatures, they like it.

 # LIBRA THE SCALES

RULER: Venus
ELEMENT: air
COLORS: blue, purple, violet
STONES: opal, pearl

YOU

POSITIVE CHARACTERISTICS

FRIENDLY AND CHARMING

Ruled by Venus, the planet of love, those born under the sign of Libra are of a friendly nature and always seem to be smiling. Surrounded by friends, the typical Libra boy will be very popular, especially with the girls. Libra girls, more than any other sign, seem to attract boys. This is because they're so happy and fun to be with. They can also be exceptionally lovely to look at and have beautiful hair. You Librans have great personal charm and few can resist your winning ways. Just smile softly, speak gently, and watch them fall over themselves trying to be with you.

GOOD JUDGEMENT AND CREATIVE

You are very creative and will have a natural ear for music. Many famous singers and musicians are born under the sign of Libra. You will love art and may be a gifted painter or sculptor. Often Librans make wonderful performing artists on the stage; the public just adore their eloquence and good looks. Psychic powers are among the many gifts given to some very sensitive Librans. Many become deeply involved in religion as a result of visionary experiences and lots of priests are born under the sign of Libra.

Librans never take anything at face value. Weighing up the odds and balancing everything out is what Libra people do best. The top careers for Librans involve assessing situations: they make excellent judges, research scientists, teachers, doctors, and surgeons.

NEGATIVE CHARACTERISTICS

OUTSPOKEN AND EMOTIONAL

If anyone really upsets a Libran, they had better watch out. You are slow to anger but when you're pushed too far you are dynamite. Your gift of sweet-talking friends is matched by your ability to cut foes to ribbons with your sharply critical tongue. You are naturally calm and well balanced but at times your emotions can overcome you. This often happens if you feel someone you love isn't responding to you, a rare occurrence but to you very painful. At times you can be too critical of other people's minor faults and you speak out when things don't seem quite right. This is because as a Libran you want everything to be properly balanced and in harmony. Unfortunately this state of perfection exists only now and again, so many of you will be forever chasing rainbows.

HEALTH

Back pains are a frequent complaint of Librans. They also have more headaches than most other signs. Some Librans can be very nervous and may not always feel like sparkling and twinkling. Not to worry, Librans are usually quite strong and have a great ability to bounce back from minor illnesses such as colds and flu.

YOUR PET

POSITIVE CHARACTERISTICS

LOVING AND GENTLE

Peaceful and very loving, Libra pets haven't got an enemy in the world, at least not for long. These pets will go to great lengths to live in harmony and hate any aggression. Shouting and loud voices upset Libra pets; they are very gentle creatures and just want to be friends. Libra dogs will never start a fight, they are too gentle for that. No Libra dog is going to be a great guard, because they are born with an instinct to befriend others.

FRIENDLY AND FLIRTY
Libra pets are all flirty things, they will cuddle up and almost ask to be loved. A typical Libra cat will have every visitor to your home trying to stroke it. A Libra dog loves nothing better than being tickled and cuddled, by anyone. They are also quick learners and easy to train.

NEGATIVE CHARACTERISTICS

ATTENTION-SEEKER
Things have got to be all sweetness and light for the Libra pet. The Libra dog will need a firm set of rules and must know exactly how far it can go. Sometimes Libra dogs try too hard to get attention and can even be destructive. The Libra cat will show its claws if someone annoys it. Be aware that Libra pets have a need to be constantly loved. If you fail to give them all the care and attention they want, they can become very demanding.

HEALTH
Libra pets can be rather lazy and need to be exercised regularly. This laziness can lead to weight gain and you must make sure they don't eat too much. Try putting your Libra pet on the scales at your vet's surgery, then check it against a weight chart. Libra cats are always ready for a snack and will eat your fish supper if you leave it unguarded.

PET TIPS
With Libra pets, love is extra important and all members of your family will be expected to show your pet affection. Most Libra animals want nothing more than peace and love — they are super pets.

 # SCORPIO THE SCORPION

RULERS: Mars and Pluto
ELEMENT: water
COLORS: red, blue
STONES: ruby, turquoise

YOU

POSITIVE CHARACTERISTICS

AMBITIOUS AND ABLE

Perhaps the most powerful of all the star signs, Scorpio gives those born under it personality plus. The typical Scorpio will have hypnotic eyes and a strong personal presence that seems almost overpowering at times. Very ambitious people are often born under Scorpio and they let nothing get in their way. Many brilliant public speakers are born under Scorpio and they seem able almost to hypnotize audiences with their words.

In love, the Scorpio is irresistible. Boys are so strong-willed and determined that they usually get the girl of their dreams. Girls born under this sign are often dramatically gifted and their desires are very strong. When a Scorpio girl decides that a boy is right for her, he will soon fall under her seemingly magical spell.

RESOURCEFUL AND INTELLIGENT

No matter how difficult a task may be, those born under Scorpio seem able to take it on and succeed.

Scorpio-sign children are frequently top of their class, often by the sheer power of their concentration. Their grasp of situations and ability almost to read people's minds comes from the mystical nature of this most positive of star signs. Many Scorpio girls have psychic powers and can sometimes sense what is going to happen before it does. Scorpio boys are usually good at sport and they play all games with great grit and determination.

Resourceful and intelligent, those born under Scorpio have the will and ability to succeed in the profession of their choice, but only if they choose it with care. Top careers usually involve sensitive creativity: producer or script writer for film or television, for example.

NEGATIVE CHARACTERISTICS

WICKED TEMPER

There is a sting in the tail of all Scorpios. Cross them and you are certain to be stung, sooner or later. This sign is very unforgiving and most people born under Scorpio insist on getting their revenge for any injury or slight. You upset a Scorpio at your peril. If you value your wellbeing, always run from any confrontation with them. At times Scorpios can be very jealous and will turn on anyone who threatens their loved ones or their home and property. Their wicked temper is frightening to see and is best avoided. If you are born under this sign, try to keep these traits in check.

HEALTH

In youth the typical Scorpio may be quite thin, but this changes around their fortieth year and they tend towards overweight in later life. Heart problems are the main source of concern, and no one born under Scorpio should smoke tobacco.

YOUR PET

POSITIVE CHARACTERISTICS

BRAVE AND LOYAL

If you want a self-motivated pet with bags of get-up-and-go, then Scorpio is the sign for you. These pets know what they want and there is little point in trying to stop them by force. The way to treat any Scorpio pet is with a good deal of respect. They are very proud creatures and like to make their own rules. A typical Scorpio dog will defend its territory to the end. Brilliant guards and wonderful, loyal friends, Scorpio dogs are all that a dog should be and a bit more on top for good measure. It is just impossible to own a Scorpio cat, but it may agree to live with you. These pets have everything you might want, twice.

GOOD MEMORY

Treat a Scorpio pet with kindness and you have a friend for life. They have long memories and never forget those who love and care for them. Conversely, it is a big, big mistake to mistreat a Scorpio pet.
They will get you for it in the end. Scorpio cats and dogs are fighters, they fear nothing and no one. This can result in trouble, since Scorpio pets, like all other pets, come in various shapes and sizes. They may not win every battle but their adversary will know they have been in a rumble.

Very clever and quick to claim territory, the Scorpio pet will assume control of your house if you let it. Be very diplomatic when you deal with any of these pets — they like to be in charge.

NEGATIVE CHARACTERISTICS

CAN BE VICIOUS

Goodness gracious me, what big teeth you have! Yes, it's Scorpio pet in a bad mood and time to go, fast. The Scorpio pet has no fear, only a very bad temper, and it will snap your hand off if you annoy it. Scorpio cats are ferocious fighters and will even take on dogs. If you hear a howling and screeching from the back garden, Scorpio cat is defending its territory. Scorpio dog will chase anyone it considers to be a threat — if one comes after you, climb a tree.

HEALTH

In a fight, the Scorpio pet will not give in and therefore often suffers quite a lot of injury when taking on a bigger foe. Like their human counterparts, Scorpio pets tend to put on weight and this must be carefully monitored.

PET TIPS

Scorpio pets are at their very best in an established routine with clear rules that they understand. They are very clever animals and will quickly learn if you teach them properly. This is essential for a happy life. The typical Scorpio pet will otherwise set out its own guidelines and enforce them. It's no use trying to bully a Scorpio pet into conforming once it has started to break house rules, so begin as you mean to go on, and you will have happy days.

SAGITTARIUS THE CENTAUR OR THE ARCHER

ELEMENT: fire
RULER: Jupiter
COLORS: purple, violet, mauve
STONES: sapphire, amethyst

YOU

POSITIVE CHARACTERISTICS

HONEST AND STRAIGHTFORWARD

As a Sagittarian you always tell the truth. You are honest, straightforward and fair in everything you do. In your work you are determined to succeed and apply your mind to any given task, ignoring distractions. Your power to think positively makes you a force to be reckoned with as you only accept success. Others find in you a friend that they can trust to speak truthfully to them.

Sagittarian boy will find the girl of his dreams and tell her straight out of his feelings for her. The girl born under this sign will be happy with her chosen love; Sagittarian girls know how to win and keep their man.

FAR-SIGHTED

The one thing Sagittarians are really good at is planning. Some think that those born under Sagittarius are gifted with powers to see the future, but this is not usually so. Typical Sagittarians think things through carefully and make the right decisions.

There is a musical side to many Sagittarians, and always a love of truth and beauty.

No one should try to guide a Sagittarian into a profession that may restrict them, for this sign thrives on change. Often very single-minded and good at school work, the Sagittarian may win many scholarships and may also be a top-class athlete. If you are a Sagittarian, be aware that if you put your mind to achieving a goal, then, with your gritty determination and hard work, you will succeed. Sagittarius is generally happiest in jobs thatinvolve travel and change. Top careers include armed-forces personnel, priest, psychiatrist, sports management.

NEGATIVE CHARACTERISTICS
BLUNT TO THE POINT OF RUDENESS

Some think that Sagittarians are rude; they are always very blunt. If you ask a Sagittarian for an opinion, you're going to get one you may not entirely like, but it will be the unedited truth. This sign is known for its very direct and often quite hurtful comments to others. If someone is wrong, the Sagittarian will tell them in no uncertain terms. This can make them quite a few enemies.

HEALTH

Muscular or rheumatic pain is frequently experienced by Sagittarians. Those born under this sign also seem to suffer from frequent sore throats. Some Sagittarians will have skin trouble, rashes, and acne.

YOUR PET
POSITIVE CHARACTERISTICS

TRUSTWORTHY

There is no such thing as a sneaky Sagittarian pet: what you see is what you get. These wonderful creatures are just endless honest fun, and they have boundless energy. A typical Sagittarius dog will chase bees round the garden on a summer's day for hours on end. Diving into muddy ponds, paw-printing your clothes and rolling in muck are also among this dog's idea of a good time. A Sagittarius cat is very brave. If you see a cat perched high up in a tree or on a rooftop, you can bet it's a Sagittarian. Don't worry about these carefree creatures and their zany antics — they are enjoying themselves and that is what Sagittarius pets do best.

FRIENDLY

Unlike their human counterparts, Sagittarian pets couldn't plan a picnic in a pet-food factory. These happy-go-lucky characters are at their fun-loving best in all sorts of trouble. Whether it involves messing up the clean carpets or chewing Dad's slippers, these pets are going to enjoy themselves. Such friendly creatures are these pets that they make lousy fighters. They think life is a game and everyone should join in. It's no use trying to tell your typical Sagittarius dog off for doing what, to it, seems perfectly natural. They can be trained but there is always a sense of adventure within them that turns everything upside down. These pets love attention, even if they have to climb a tree to get it.

NEGATIVE CHARACTERISTICS

DESTRUCTIVE

Clumsy and often very careless, these pets will rubbish your home for the fun of it. There is no point in being angry, they won't know why you don't just join in and rip a few cushions with them. If you dislike coming home to what looks like a battlefield, you had better not get a Sagittarian pet.

HEALTH

These crazy pets often injure themselves falling off things — trees, roofs, the back of your sofa. The Sagittarian dog is also likely to chase cars, motorbikes and anything that moves. This is a dangerous game but they don't care. Cats get stuck in tiny spaces where they went on some half-baked adventure; hamsters disappear under beds — you name it, these pets are up to it. Buy some good veterinary-care insurance!

PET TIPS

Get a sense of humour, fast. If you own one of these loony pets, then you have my sympathy. We love them but what can be done? Take them for very long walks, tire them out. Train them early, give them lots of attention and stand by for action. You have been warned.

 # CAPRICORN THE GOAT

ELEMENT: earth
RULER: Saturn
COLORS: violet, gray, purple
STONES: pearl, amethyst

YOU

POSITIVE CHARACTERISTICS

THOUGHTFUL AND SENSIBLE

Your ability to grasp a problem and find a solution is second to none. You are a deep thinker and have a natural ability to reason things through. Others think you are the most sensible person around and often you are asked to be in charge of things. The one thing you really look up to is knowledge: you seek information and prize it above gold.

The Capricorn boy will always take his time in selecting the right girl to be his very special one. These boys love with all their heart and are gentle and kind. A Capricorn girl will search the world to find her Mr Right. When she does, it is a forever kind of love.

INDEPENDENT AND AMBITIOUS

The very idea of doing exactly as you're told makes your blood boil. As a Capricorn you know just what you are going to do, so tell whoever is trying to push you around to get lost. They will let you get on with it eventually, because even your boss or teacher will soon realize that you are in charge of your own destiny. The typical Capricorn is very independent and needs to be in control of things. You are well equipped to make decisions and do so without fear because you just know that you're right. Everything you do will be done in a responsible and down-to- earth way. You are ambitious, you have a dream, but you are not a dreamer. Others respect your level- headed judgement and will look to you for leadership in times of trouble. If you are not in total charge in your present position, don't worry — you will be! You are a Capricorn and they think their way to the top.

The top career areas for those born under Capricorn involve thoughtful leadership skills: politics and government, business administration, estate or personal management.

NEGATIVE CHARACTERISTICS

BOSSY

Let's face it, you have an attitude problem. As far as you're concerned, you are in charge and if the others don't like it, that's their tough luck. This is not the best way to win friends, is it? Try to imagine yourself in their place and don't order them about so much. However, if you are a typical Capricorn you won't really care what others think, as long as they do what you say.

HEALTH

Sports injuries, especially to the feet and knees, are often a problem for Capricorn. You hurt yourself trying too hard, and may get muscular pains in your legs when running. This sign sometimes has trouble with indigestion and should keep a well-balanced diet with plenty of fibre.

YOUR PET

POSITIVE CHARACTERISTICS

DIGNIFIED

There is a sense of dignity about pets born under the sign of Capricorn. They have a definite air of authority about them and seem extremely confident. There is, however, a tendency for certain of these pets to assume that they're in charge. It will be the Capricorn cat that gets the cream first, for these are very smart felines indeed. You can spot the Capricorn dog: it's the one that has its tail in the air and a self-assured look on its face. Very good guard dogs are often born under this sign. However, all Capricorn pets are very loving and need human contact.

HOME-LOVING

Give a Capricorn pet a clean bed, good food and lots of love and it will be the pet of your dreams. The Capricorn cat is very home-loving and likes nothing better than being next to its owners in a happy household. Capricorn dogs love a regular routine; given this, they are wonderful house pets. All Capricorn pets are sensitive to the emotions of their owners and will know instinctively whether you are sad or happy. These pets are great game players and want you to throw a ball, chuck a stick, or just roll them about on the floor. With attention these pets seem to glow with pride; if neglected, they will sulk. They are quite psychic and will not take to some people — you can draw your own conclusions from this.

NEGATIVE CHARACTERISTICS

MOODY

Often Capricorn pets are quite moody. They have a highly developed sixth sense and if they think some major change is about to take place in the home, they will worry and sulk. Pack your bags for a holiday and watch your Capricorn dog hide away in a corner and put its paws over its eyes, and your Capricorn cat become aloof and pointedly ignore you.

These pets are also quite difficult to train. A Capricorn cat will do only what it wants to do, but the Capricorn dog responds to a regular routine. Give them a special cuddle when they behave, and they'll be fine.

HEALTH

In some households the Capricorn pet will feel threatened. This most often occurs when there are lots of family members and the pet can't establish any kind of control over its own little life. Capricorn pets tend to worry a lot and do need more reassurance than most other signs.

PET TIPS

With Capricorn dogs, training must start early and be continued for longer than usual. The cat needs to know that it is a member of a household and there are others who live in it as well. These pets like to have control over as much as possible; they will pinch your favorite chair to let you know that they can do what they want. Don't worry about it — these pets love you, and who could really ask for anything more?

AQUARIUS
THE WATER BEARER

ELEMENT: air
RULER: Uranus
COLORS: bright blue, silver gray
STONES: pink topaz, moonstone

YOU

POSITIVE CHARACTERISTICS

GOOD COMPANY

The one thing all Aquarians are is good company. They have dozens of friends and seem able to get along with almost everyone. The Aquarius boy will have so many girl friends he won't be able to pick the right one. Because this is such an outgoing sign, both boys and girls will be spoilt for choice, but the Aquarius girl is less of a flirt. She will know the boy she likes as soon as she sees him.

Your personality sparkles in company and others think you witty and great fun. Quite often those born under Aquarius will be very inventive and have a wonderful imagination.

GREAT POTENTIAL

Aquarians tend to be rather offbeat in their attitude to life. All Aquarians have a deep need to achieve and those born under this sign can go right to the very top of any chosen profession. There is great potential within the Aquarius make-up. No other sign has quite such a wide spread of ability — outstanding Aquarians range from great poets to military generals. Strong-minded in debate and always quite sure of themselves, Aquarians can be kept from the top only by a lack of determination. They frequently lose the will to see things through and end up being bested by lesser mortals. No need to worry at all; calmly decide what you really, really want, make a plan to get it and go ahead. You have friends who will help you — just look around and

35

ask them.

As well as creative, your mind is very scientific and you're always testing out theories as well as people. Top career fields for Aquarians include science, medicine, and theatre.

NEGATIVE CHARACTERISTICS
STUBBORN AND SOMETIMES WEIRD
Once you make up your mind, you just won't change it, will you? No matter what everyone else tells you, you are an Aquarius and you go your own way. If others are less than you expect them to be, then you ignore them. Your outlook on life is eccentric, and your taste in clothes and music can be quite bizarre and designed to provoke. As for being reliable, well, you're about as reliable as sunshine on a holiday weekend. Only you know why you are such a weirdo. One day you may grow out of it but, if you are a typical Aquarian, it won't be in this lifetime.

HEALTH
Bad eyesight seems to trouble many born under the sign of Aquarius. There is also some tendency for the older Aquarian to suffer from circulatory problems.

YOUR PET

POSITIVE CHARACTERISTICS
INTERESTING AND DIFFERENT
The Aquarius pet seems to go out of its way to be different. If you have a dog that sits quietly in a corner until your dinner is served, then starts bouncing off the walls, you probably have an Aquarius pet. The cats are just as unpredictable: one minute they're contentedly purring and preening themselves, the next they're on the table snatching your chicken leg. No way can you tame an Aquarius pet. They sometimes pretend to be safe and ordinary, but under that calm exterior bubbles the excitement waiting to erupt. If your rabbit seems gentle and playful one second and mad as a March hare the next, it's ten to one you own an Aquarius bunny. These nonconformist creatures are possibly the most interesting pets of all.

VERY ATTRACTIVE

No matter whether you own a dog, a cat, or a lizard, if it's an Aquarius, it will be the best-looking pet in town. Many people will admire your pet, and you can tell that it knows very well how pretty it is. These pets are also very social creatures and will get along well with most people. A typical Aquarius
dog will even befriend a cat, and these dogs rarely start fights. Anyone who picks on them, though, will soon regret it, for they don't like to be beaten.

Aquarius is such an unpredictable sign that your pet might very well not fit this description. Or it could just change from day to day and hour to hour. You never really know with an Aquarius pet. Great fun, though!

NEGATIVE CHARACTERISTICS

A BIT SELFISH AT TIMES

Aquarius pets not only like to have all their own way, they insist on it. A typical Aquarius dog will have its own idea of doing things and neither you nor the rest of the world can change that. The general outlook of all Aquarius pets is best summed up as 'Who cares what you think?' They can seem selfish but deep inside they are much happier when they have settled into a family. This often takes quite some time as their crazy behaviour creates confusion in even the most disordered of homes.

HEALTH

Feeding Aquarius pets can be a problem. One day they like a certain type of food, the next they won't touch it. Regular exercise is essential for all pets and especially for these.

PET TIPS

Try to get your pet to recognize the area it is allowed in. If you don't do this as soon as you get an Aquarius-sign pet, it will very soon be everywhere. Cats should be lifted off the table whenever they climb on. Speak very firmly but ever so sweetly to these pets. It's no use trying to force them to do anything — they'll do exactly the opposite if you try that.

PISCES THE FISHES

ELEMENT: water
RULERS: Neptune and Jupiter
COLORS: violet, mauve, purple
STONES: emerald, agate, sapphire

YOU

POSITIVE CHARACTERISTICS

GENEROUS AND LOYAL

As a Piscean you will want to listen to other people's problems and help them. You are very loyal to your friends and others trust you with their innermost secrets. The Pisces boy will have every lonely girl in school confiding in him; they just love to talk to such a good listener. The Pisces girl makes every young man's dream come true as she places all her hope and trust in her extra-special partner. There is a very generous side to the Piscean nature and they are generally kind, gentle, and loving people.

PSYCHIC, CHARMING, AND QUICK-WITTED

Psychic powers are part of the make-up of many Pisces people. These can give them the ability to see beyond the public face worn by many as a mask to disguise their true selves. Others will say that you can 'see right through them'. True Pisceans use their gifts for the benefit of others and are charming and often funny, with a quick wit. Very complex but great fun to be with, you will always be popular, a real party animal.

Pisces people seem to just know things that they have never studied. Many geniuses and people with amazing abilities are Piscean. Comedians and great actors are often born under the sign of Pisces. They have some advantage over other signs as the psychic side of their nature gives them a real insight. In front of an audience the Pisces character shines out like a bright light. Because the typical Piscean has a dual or double nature, they find it easy to act out a part. However, some may think that you are acting all the time when you're being your true self, whoever that may be. Other top careers for Pisces people involve travel and/or interpersonal skills; for example, psychologist or counsellor, sailor, pop- group manager.

NEGATIVE CHARACTERISTICS

CHANGEABLE

No one can quite work you out. Like the wind, you blow this way and that. Those close to you consider you to be a total mystery. You can make decisions quite quickly, then you have a little think and change your mind. This can cause others to wonder what you are playing at. It isn't that you mean to be difficult, you just dive in head first, look about and start swimming in the opposite direction. Is there something fishy about this? Of course there is, you are ruled by Pisces.

HEALTH

Sleeping problems often disturb Pisces people, probably because of their very vivid dreams. Stomach troubles can occur. This sign should never smoke tobacco.

YOUR PET

POSITIVE CHARACTERISTICS

MYSTERIOUS

The dreamers of the pet world are born under the sign of Pisces. These pets will sit and stare into space for ages. They are the most sensitive of pets and will instantly know if their owner is ill or upset You can count on these pets to bring you comfort in any time of need.

The Pisces cat seems to be a hundred different characters rolled into one. Sometimes they're really smart and can open fridge doors, lift the tuna steak, then close it behind them. Other times they can't even locate their own feed bowl. All Pisces pets are a mystery to their owners.

PSYCHIC

If you have a dog that runs for its lead the minute you think about going walkies, the odds are it's a psychic Pisces pet. Cats born under this sign seem to be almost supernatural creatures. They love the darkness and midnight is their favorite hour. Watch your Pisces pets when the Moon is full: there is a lunar side to this sign and these are definitely creatures of the night. Some Piscean dogs are so in tune with the phases of the Moon that they howl like the wolves their ancestors once were.

These psychic pets are really lovable and happy animals, very much in harmony with their owners. If you own a Pisces pet, let it dream — the chances are it is dreaming about you.

NEGATIVE CHARACTERISTICS

LONER

The typical Pisces pet likes nothing better than to be left alone. You may think that they are ignoring you but this is not so. They know exactly what's going on and just choose to opt out and dream. The Pisces dog will never be a great guard: it may stare at the intruder with moony eyes but actually tearing the seat out of their trousers is far too much trouble. You Pisces cat will often take itself off into the moonlit night without a thought for you or anyone else.

Pisces pets are usually very gentle. They love you but some rarely show their affection.

HEALTH

Living in a world of their own, these pets can be rather withdrawn at times and go off their food. Sometimes their night-time wanderings get them into trouble with the neighbours. Your Pisces pets will be members of the local cats' choir or doggy Moon- howling circle, so look out for boot marks on their backsides.

PET TIPS

Give these dreamy pets something nice to dream about. Lots of little treats go down well when training. Always respect their psychic powers. You can tune in to these telepathic pets, who are already tuned in to you. Be happy and they will be happy. But they're not to be messed with when the Moon is full and the wind is in the west.

STAR-SIGN ASSESSMENTS
YOU AND YOUR PET

The following two assessment tests have been specially designed to check whether you and your pet are typical of your star signs. All you have to do is read each statement very carefully and place a tick in the box next to the ten statements that best describe you.

At the end of the test, just note the numbers of the ten statements you have ticked and refer to the assessment chart.

It is quite possible that you don't feel you have many of the characteristics of your star sign. This may be because some other aspect of your birth chart predominates. To find out more about this, refer to the section on astro-dowsing.

Have a giggle as you fill these assessments in, but don't think of them as a blueprint for your life. Always bear in mind that the world loves a trier. Do your best in life and in the end you will succeed.

YOUR STAR-SIGN ASSESSMENT TEST

You may select **ONLY TEN** statements from the following list of 50. Remember there are negative as well as positive sides to all our characters. Place a tick in the box alongside the ten statements that you think most closely describe you, your character and your attitude to life. To get the best from this assessment, don't look at the answers first!

1) Your outstanding mind and brilliant brain are only matched by your great modesty.[ ]

2) Others consider you fun to be with and you have lots of friends [ ]

3) Given a problem you can soon find an answer, and you are very logical [ ]

4) You are a truthful and honest person, trusted by others [ ]

5) You are teacher's pet, they keep you in a cage at the back of the classroom [ ]

6) You are generally a happy individual who tries to look on the bright side of life [ ]

7) You can instantly recall many facts and figures [ ]

8) You have great determination and will to win [ ]

9) You like to keep your room neat and tidy [ ]

10) Some say you have a magnetic personality [ ]

11) You are always certain of your ability to do things.[ ]

12) You love material things — clothes, cars, computers [ ]

13) You have a good ability to remember jokes and tell them well [ ]

14) You are the flirty type, have lots of boy/girl friends and suffer from headaches [ ]

15) Some people think you're big-headed, a bit of a show-off. [ ]
16) At school you are the one whose homework is most often copied. [ ]
17) There are always lots of friends around — aren't you the popular one! [ ]
18) Your idea of hard work is getting out of bed before noon. [ ]
19) Others think you have hypnotic powers. [ ]
20) Many trust your judgement and you make considered decisions.[ ]
21) You like to organize things, and others expect you to take charge [ ]
22) You're quite a gifted writer and your stories are read out in class [ ]
23) You are very loyal to your friends and keep the secrets they tell you [ ]
24) You have a very inventive mind and can think up a good excuse for anything [ ]
25) You're happiest in a comfortable home with good food and friends [ ]
26) You are able to see the faults in others and sometimes point these out [ ]
27) You are quite possessive and would like your boy/girl friend with you all the time [ ]
28) You find it very difficult to believe that you are wrong, ever [ ]
29) You like being scruffy and wear the same smelly old trainers every day [ ]
30) Your ability to think clearly has earned you top marks in your school work. [ ]
31) You are very sensitive and some think you have psychic powers[ ]
32) You enjoy travel and your parents want you to go round the world, at once [ ]
33) You consider yourself to be totally in charge of your own destiny [ ]
34) You are really way out and weird at times [ ]
35) You have flashes of inspiration and some think you are a genius [ ]
36) Nothing gets in your way, you're very single- minded. [ ]
37) You are very poetic and read many of the great writers for pleasure [ ]

38) Your idea of a good time involves collecting train numbers and used bus tickets.[ ]

39) You can outwit most others [ ]

40) You can sense when people are telling you lies [ ]

41) You hate to fail and you will never accept defeat [ ]

42) You are wide awake to tricksters and no one pulls the wool over your eyes [ ]

43) You have a good ability to weigh situations up and consider all the options [ ]

44) You speak to trees, flowers, and grass, and sometimes they reply [ ]

45) You are a clear and very clever speaker, others listen to you [ ]

46) You tell others the truth even though this may be hurtful [ ]

47) You like to be in command of situations and will quickly take control [ ]

48) Once you make your mind up no one can change it [ ]

49) No one can ever quite work you out, one minute this, next minute that [ ]

50) You can balance building bricks and are the smartest kid in the secure unit [ ]

YOUR PET'S STAR-SIGN
ASSESSMENT TEST

You may select ONLY FIVE statements from the following list of 30. Remember there are positive and negative sides to all star signs. Place a tick in the box alongside the five statements that you think most closely describe your pet. To get the best from this assessment, don't look at the answers first!

1) Your pet seems to be a bit of a dreamer and likes staring at the Moon [ ]

2) Your pet likes watching TV, especially the football [ ]

3) A most attractive pet, widely admired.....[ ]

4) Very dignified and self-assured. [ ]

5) This pet likes mail carriers and other strangers, uncooked, alive, and screaming [ ]

6) A happy-go-lucky pet that is into all sorts of mischief.[ ]

7) Quite determined pet that will not hesitate to fight back if

provoked [ ]

8) Peaceful, calm, and contented, a really lovable pet.[ ]

9) A refined pet with aristocratic ideals, insists on a silver service at mealtimes [ ]

10) A very clever pet, this character doesn't need teaching things twice. [ ]

11) This pet thinks it is in charge, a really bossy character with bags of swagger [ ]

12) A pet that can read your mind or seems to be in tune with you [ ]

13) This pet switches its affection from one to another almost daily [ ]

14) A crafty pet, this character cheats at cards and plays with a tooth-marked deck.[ ]

15) Loves its toys and guards them fiercely [ ]

16) A stubborn pet that will only do exactly what it wants to do [ ]

17) This pet seems to know when its time for a treat and jumps up in expectation [ ]

18) Calm and collected one minute, crazy the next — an unpredictable pet.[ ]

19) There is a real air of authority about this noble creature [ ]

20) This pet is a real show-off and will dance the hokey-cokey to get attention.[ ]

21) A rather clumsy pet, often falls off things it shouldn't be on in the first place [ ]

22) A very protective pet that will guard you and your property against any attack.[ ]

23) No one can resist stroking this friendly and gentle creature [ ]

24) A very clean pet, will not touch food unless it is served in a clean bowl. [ ]

25) This pet can't be moved from your favourite chair [ ]

26) This pet likes to play rough and is very strong [ ]

27) A really affectionate pet, welcomes you home with a wagging tail and a lick [ ]

28) Soon gets bored and likes to play lots of different games..[ ]

29) Likes a lot of exercise and is big and powerful for its breed. [ ]

30) A very active pet that lives life at a fast pace, can be accident prone [ ]

YOUR PERSONAL ASSESSMENT

Note the ten numbers that you have identified and check these against those given alongside your star sign. If you have all five of the numbers given, then you are very typical, but you may find a cluster under another sign that also influences your personality.

ARIES the ram: 3. 11. 36. 43. 46.

TAURUS the Bull: 10. 12. 22. 25. 37.

GEMINI the Twins: 3. 13. 26. 39. 49.

CANCER the Crab: 9. 14. 27. 31. 40.

LEO the Lion: 8. 15. 28. 36. 41.

VIRGO the Virgin: 7. 16. 30. 42. 43.

LIBRA the Scales: 6. 17. 31. 40. 43.

SCORPIO the Scorpion: 8. 10. 19. 31. 45.

SAGITTARIUS the Centaur /Archer: 3. 4. 20. 32. 45.

CAPRICORN the Goat: 3. 21. 33. 43. 47.

AQUARIUS the Water Bearer: 2. 22. 34. 35. 48.

PISCES the Fishes: 17. 23. 35. 45. 49.

If your numbers don't turn up under any of these, you must have been born off-planet.

YOUR PET'S PERSONAL ASSESSMENT

Note the five numbers that you have identified and check these against those given alongside your pet's star sign. If your pet has all three of the numbers given, it's very typical of its sign. But if it's not, well, pets, like people, are all individuals and it would be a strange hamster that was a great and ferocious guard.

ARIES the Ram: 16. 27. 30.

TAURUS the Bull: 15. 22. 29.

GEMINI the Twins: 13. 18. 28.

CANCER the Crab: 8. 12. 27.

LEO the Lion: 11. 22. 26.

VIRGO the Virgin: 10. 19. 24.
LIBRA the Scales: 3. 8. 23.
SCORPIO the Scorpion: 7. 22. 29.
SAGITTARIUS the Centaur or Archer: 6. 21. 30.
CAPRICORN the Goat: 4. 10. 28.
AQUARIUS the Water Bearer: 3. 18. 29.
PISCES the Fishes: 1. 17. 27.

Your pet's numbers not here?   Perhaps it's a cyberpet.

ASTRO-NUMBERS

LUCKY NUMBERS FOR YOU AND YOUR PET

The power of numbers was important to the wise ones of old, who believed that each person and creature on the planet Earth had a series of numbers that brought them luck and good fortune. Yours would be, for example, the numbers associated with the date on which you were born and the stars and planets that have influence over you. Now, by looking at the tables below and using the unique Astro-Dowsing Chart (page 4), you and your pet can discover the magical numbers that bring luck into your lives.

BIRTH-DATE ASTRO-NUMBERS

A very simple way of discovering one of the lucky numbers for you or your pet is to look at the day of birth. Below is a list from 1 to 9 that corresponds with the days of the months. If you were born on the 21st, just add 2 + 1 which equals 3: this is one of your lucky numbers as it is directly related to the day of your birth.

NUMBER 1: all those born on 1st, 10th, 19th, 28th.
NUMBER 2: all those born on 2nd, 11th, 20th, 29th.
NUMBER 3: all those born on 3rd, 12th, 21st, 30th.
NUMBER 4: all those born on 4th, 13th, 22nd, 31st.
NUMBER 5: all those born on 5th, 14th, 23rd.
NUMBER 6: all those born on 6th, 15th, 24th.
NUMBER 7: all those born on 7th, 16th, 25th.
NUMBER 8: all those born on 8th, 17th, 26th.
NUMBER 9: all those born on 9th, 18th, 27th.

Each of these prime numbers brings a special power to those that are born within its period of influence. To discover the forces present within your own and your pet's numbers, just refer to the relevant astro-numbers below.

ASTRO-NUMBER CHARACTERISTICS

Having discovered your own or your pet's number, now read the assessment of the influences present within
its power.

THE NUMBER 1

PLANET: the Sun
LUCKY DAYS: Sunday, Monday
LUCKY COLORS: gold, yellow, bronze
LUCKY JEWELS/STONES: topaz, amber
LUCKY HEALTH-BRINGING FOOD: oranges, raisins, dates

YOU

Very creative people are born under the influence of the number 1. It is the beginning, the first number, and it is the base from which everything else flows. You will have a vivid imagination, be a writer, a poet, or a visionary, maybe an inventor. Your mind
knows no boundaries and above all you want to be different. You love dressing in a way that draws attention. Your clothes are bright and yellow is one of your favorite colors. Like the Sun that gives power to this number, you shine like a bright light in life. Members of the opposite sex find you very attractive because you're so self-assured and positive. You will be very proud, sometimes too much so. You love being in the spotlight; in fact, you're a bit of a show-off. You can't help it, you're a number-1 person, so enjoy yourself!

PERSONAL TIPS

Try to put your natural creative ability to good use. Write poems, stories, invent things, and always remember: you're number 1, so be the best! Never be a big brag, let your talent do the talking. Everyone knows you're brilliant, so shine on, you number 1, you!

YOUR PET

Talk about attention-seeking pets and you must be talking about those born under the influence of number 1. Number-1 cats can't get enough cuddles and will sit on your knee for hours, so long as you tickle and stroke them. A number-1 dog is probably the friendliest, most loving woofer of them all. These number-1 pets are really very soft, they want you to love them all the time. If your pet is a typical number 1, then lucky old you, if you like snuggles, cuddles, and tickle-me-tum-tum day and night. Very easy-going, home-loving and most of all friendly, the number-1 pet is every owner's best pal.

PET TIP

Number-1 dogs never make good guards. They would roll over for a tickle from even the most horrible robber, so forget that idea. Number-1 cats need lots of attention, so if you can't give this to them, expect a pussy with a long face because they will sulk.

THE NUMBER 2

PLANET: the Moon
LUCKY DAYS: Monday, Friday
LUCKY COLORS: silver, pale green, cream
LUCKY JEWELS/STONES: pearl, emerald, moonstone
LUCKY HEALTH-BRINGING FOOD: melons, lettuce, turnips

YOU

You are gentle and very artistic. You're romantic and often fall in love too quickly. Others see you as a dreamer but you can make all your dreams come true because as a number-2 person you have imagination. You can be very sensitive to the comments of others, but there is no need to be, you know what is right and are very psychic. Your main strength is in your power to think ahead and plan. Business managers and public officials are very often number-2 people. There is an almost visionary power to your planning and somehow you seem to get things just right. Others think you're a bit spooky at times. Your lovelife may involve many passionate affairs as you seek for that one very special person. Dream on, number-2, and make those dreams come true!

PERSONAL TIPS

Be positive about your life and start each day determined to succeed. You have a real talent to imagine situations you would like to achieve — well, get on and make it happen! Always remember that you have a special sixth sense, you know deep inside what to do, so wakey-wakey, number-2, and get on with it!

YOUR PET

Sleepy-time pets, that is probably the best way to describe those born under the influence of this Moon- struck number. If your pet likes nothing better than a good snooze and a snore, then it is quite likely a gentle number 2. These are very sensitive creatures and have a mystical side to their nature. Being ruled by the Moon, many number-2 pets will have psychic powers and may even be able to read your mind. These pets will be waiting by their food bowl the minute you think about feeding them. They can be rather lonely if they don't get lots of attention.

PET TIPS

Number-2 pets have a real need to be loved and made a fuss of. They will think you don't care if they aren't cuddled at least once a day. You should also talk to them, because they seem to be able to understand. Think in images as you speak: if talking to your dog about a walk, picture this in your mind, then watch it jump for joy. These are very gentle and loving pets, but a number-2 dog is no softie. They will guard their property and their friends. Watch these pets when the wind blows in from the west and the Moon is full — they are lunar-tuned.

THE NUMBER 3

PLANET: Jupiter
LUCKY DAYS: Tuesday, Thursday
LUCKY COLORS: orange, turquoise, blue
LUCKY JEWEL/STONE: amethyst
LUCKY HEALTH-BRINGING FOOD: beetroot, wheat

YOU

Very independent and only really happy when you are in control of any situation. You do not hesitate to take charge and others accept your authority, often without question. You can take as well as give orders; in occupations like the armed forces you shine out as an example to others. Self-discipline is one of the strong points of a number-3 person. There is a powerful will inside you that drives you on to success. Very ambitious and clear-sighted, you know where you're going and won't let things get in the way. You need a degree of freedom in your life and will never be tied down in some boring everyday job. Naturally adventurous, you will take chances to get to the top, which is where all number-3 people aim at. If you're a real number-3 individual, you will love a challenge.

PERSONAL TIPS

Try to keep a close eye on your target when aiming for some goal. One problem often experienced by number-3 people is aiming beyond their abilities. Try to be realistic as well as adventurous. There is also a tendency for you to give orders in such a way that others feel threatened. Try to be less of the big boss! We all know you're in charge, so we don't need it rubbed up our noses, do we?

YOUR PET

Happy-go-lucky and playful pets are often born under the power of number 3. There is a sense of fun about these creatures and if your pet likes to play ball, fetch a stick, and run rings round you, then you've probably got a number 3. One little problem with a number 3 is that they like playing so much, they don't care who with. These are not one-person pets, they are the playboys and playgirls of the pet world. Very flirty pets, they have lots of pals.

These pets like to learn things and have the ability to master all sorts of tricks. They will know exactly where their lead is and need to be shown only once to find their box or sleeping place.

PET TIPS

Number-3 pets need more food than most other numbers. They burn energy at a very fast rate. These creatures want a lot of exercise and are at their very best when given it. If you have a number-3 dog, long walks are the order of every day. Number-3 cats will be off on the tiles at every opportunity and hate to be kept in, unless you're playing with them. These are highly active pets, so make sure they have plenty of good food and clean water.

THE NUMBER 4

PLANET: Uranus
LUCKY DAYS: Monday, Saturday
LUCKY COLORS: electric blue, shocking pink, scarlet
LUCKY JEWEL/STONE: sapphire
LUCKY HEALTH-BRINGING FOOD: spinach, grapes

YOU

Rebels and original thinkers are usually born under the power of number 4. These people seem to be very argumentative and fall out with others for no good reason. To their close friends number-4 types are kind and understanding, but everyone else can go and take a flying jump. The idea that something is crazy or impossible just makes these people more determined to do it. Look for number 4 on the flying trapeze or climbing a steep mountain. With wonderful imaginations, number-4 people are full of ideas. Be aware that they are destined for glory, unless disaster stops them on the way.

PERSONAL TIPS

There's not much point really: if you're a number 4, you're not going to pay any attention to this, so best let you get on with it. However, just in case you're still reading, here is where you may go wrong on your journey into the history books. You are always too ready to take the opposite view and never stop to think that there may be a better way of doing things. Obeying rules and regulations may not be your favourite way of getting things done, but think of the trouble you will create by ignoring them. You don't care, do you? Best of luck!

YOUR PET

Want a pet of outrageous character? Then pick a number 4. They will usually be the ones that do exactly the opposite of what you expect. On a rainy day the number-4 dog will insist on the longest walk of the week. If it's sunny and clear, it'll want to sleep. The number-4 cat is one of the greatest of all mysteries: just where they go for days on end is anyone's guess. These are original pets, they have their way of doing things and you might as well let them get on with it. Conforming to your routine is just out of the question, and they often seem not to know what they want themselves. They are, however, great fun. Playing games with a number-4 pet is an experience in itself. They will fetch the stick or ball one minute, then run off and hide it the next. They are playing by their own rules, so join in and enjoy it.

PET TIPS

You should try to train your number-4 pet at a very early age. "Try" is the right word — you'll be lucky to succeed. Keep lots of different foods for them, because they change their minds almost daily on what they do and don't like to eat.

THE NUMBER 5

PLANET: Mercury
LUCKY DAYS: Wednesday, Friday
LUCKY COLORS: silver, pearl gray, light green
LUCKY JEWEL/STONE: diamond
LUCKY HEALTH-BRINGING FOOD: carrots, oats

YOU

Intelligent and very sharp-witted, the number-5 person sees clearly the mistakes that others miss. Often extremely clever and naturally charming, number-5 people are real winners. Sometimes they dazzle others with their brilliant minds, and they can rise very quickly to the top in group situations. Others look to these clear thinkers to examine their plans or work for faults. There is, however, a tendency for some to be overcritical, and their outspoken, direct way of telling others that they're wrong can sometimes be hurtful. These people are often very gifted writers or speakers and will always have a good grasp of the facts. No other number is as resilient as number 5; these people bounce back from all sorts of problems that would destroy lesser mortals. Very hard workers with careful and highly organized minds, those born under the number 5 are often the real power behind the scenes. They are simply too smart to get pushed to the front. Fives will survive — they're cool.

PERSONAL TIPS

Well, I was thinking of asking you! Your ability to grasp the essentials of any situation should enable you to succeed where others fail. All you have to do is remain very calm — you do tend to become extra excited as success approaches. Try not to sneer at lesser mortals, they are not so gifted as you and might take offence at your insults. Be kind, gentle, and diplomatic in all your dealings with people, and you will one day be exactly where you want to be.

YOUR PET

If your pet seems to think that it owns you, then the chances are it is a number 5. These wonderful creatures get on with their little lives, sure that everything is going to be fine. You may try to teach them tricks and end up being taught some instead. These are clever pets with bags of personality and charm. They never seem sad, no matter what happens. If you're ever feeling ill and your pet comes and cuddles you, you can bet it's a number 5. These are very caring pets and are happiest when sitting next to their owners.

PET TIPS

These clever pets should be given plenty to think about. Try letting them select their favourite food from a series of different brands. Just put one out and watch as your pet eats it: if your pet is particularly happy with the meal, it will let you know. These pets may not be able to speak but they have a way of getting you to understand their likes and dislikes. One thing all number-5 pets love is a night-night cuddle. Lucky you!

THE NUMBER 6

PLANET: Venus
LUCKY DAYS: Thursday, Friday
LUCKY COLORS: pastel shades, blue, pink, green
LUCKY JEWEL/STONE: turquoise
LUCKY HEALTH-BRINGING FOOD: melons, beans

YOU

You are probably the most popular party guest in town. Your wit and your charming ways make you the centre of attraction, which is what you like being best of all.

The number-6 person will have lots of friends and always seems to be happy. One thing these fun-loving types do not like is arguments, they prefer harmony and happiness. Often very generous, number-6

people will not let their friends down. They seem to think
they have a duty to fight the battles of those close to them. They are
also very tough and won't give in once engaged in any struggle. They
love life and will help anyone: that is one of their big weaknesses as
some do exploit these kind souls.

Often number-6 people are very talented writers or artists with a
strong sentimental side to their work. They are usually romantic and
may be dreamers, but these dreams can come true.

PERSONAL TIPS

Try to be less extreme in your personal life. Often you get too
enthusiastic and go totally overboard. This will create some difficult
situations for you, as, once in the deep end, you have to climb out. Let
others fight their own battles for a change. Lots of people are too ready
to come to you and expect you to finish a fight they started.   We
know you want to help, but choose your good causes with care. And
stop and think of yourself from time to time. Remember you have a
great talent — use it to your best advantage!

YOUR PET

If your pet is at its happiest outdoors in the garden or some nearby
wood, then you can bet its number is 6. These friendly creatures just
love being close to nature and are fond of rolling in the grass or
splashing through some sweet singing stream. The number-6 dog will
often charge into woodland on a wild chase after invisible enemies and
emerge covered in mud and twigs. The cat of this nature-loving
number will curl content beside you on a picnic, then suddenly run off
after some unseen creature. Pets of this number are thought by some to
see the fairies, elves, and gnomes that are supposed to live in the green
undergrowth. Observe your pet when out with it in the woods. If you
see it stare into some clearing in the trees, it may be seeing elemental
spirits where you only see mushrooms. These number-6 pets are very
gentle creatures, at their best when given lots of exercise out in the
fields.

PET TIPS

Number-6 pets sometimes get into trouble when out in the woods and
fields. Keep them extra clean, properly vaccinated, and look out for
ticks and minor injuries. Lots of outdoor fun!

THE NUMBER 7

PLANET: Neptune
LUCKY DAYS: Sunday, Monday
LUCKY COLORS: green, white, yellow
LUCKY JEWELS/STONES: moonstone, pearl
LUCKY HEALTH-BRINGING FOOD: apples, lettuce

YOU

The typical number-7 person will love to travel and see the world. This number has to move on; they are never happy just living an ordinary life in an ordinary town. These number-7 types seem to be gifted with mystical powers and may be very psychic. They are frequently brilliant actors or public speakers and have an almost hypnotic hold over an audience. Many explorers and sailors are born under the power of number 7. It is the most restless force and many seem driven to journey from country to country, searching and seeking they know not what. Very often the number-7 individual will become involved in a religious movement, but always this is obscure or out of the ordinary. There is nothing ordinary whatsoever about the number-7 person — they are a complete mystery to all who try to know them. Deep, dark, and interesting. Goodbye is their favourite word.

PERSONAL TIPS

You are a very sensitive person but tend to hide these feelings as you move on from place to place, leaving broken hearts behind. Try to understand that there are those that love you deeply and your constant need for change upsets them. They hate to see you go, but go you will — you must! It is the nature of your number. Just remember to telephone or write. If it were you being left behind, your heart would ache too, so be gentle. You are not alone.

YOUR PET

Sensitive soulmate pets are usually born under the number-7. These loving and very gentle creatures want nothing more than to be your friend. They are also very loyal and if you look after and love a number-7 pet, it will never forget you.

These pets particularly need to feel secure. There is something in the nature of number 7 that makes pets very home-loving. If you have a friendly pet that likes nothing better than to curl up in its box or sleeping quarters, then you can bet it's a number 7. The dog born under this number will be a great guard — it loves its home and won't let anyone in that it mistrusts. The number-7 cat has its own little area; you will see it snuggled up in the same place every day, safe and contented.

PET TIPS

Make your number-7 pet feel at home. They sometimes worry that you don't love them, so show them lots and lots of affection. These pets are at their best in their own space, so make it as comfortable as you can. For a real home-loving pal, no one could do better that have a number-7 pet. Remember always to tell them not to worry if you go out.

THE NUMBER 8

PLANET: Saturn
LUCKY DAYS: Saturday, Sunday
LUCKY COLORS: gray, black, purple
LUCKY JEWELS/STONES: amethyst, dark sapphire
LUCKY HEALTH-BRINGING FOOD: celery, carrots

YOU

People of destiny are often born under the power of the number 8. Fate seems to play a great part in their life and many will lead very public and extraordinary lives. If you're a number-8 person, you will feel both ambitious and certain of your abilities. There is a strong sense of purpose to this dynamic and powerful number, which helps those under its influence to succeed. Others will trust your judgement as you seem able to advise with a wisdom beyond your years. It is as though you instinctively know things that are hidden to others. Many number-8 people will find they are living in two different worlds: one where they are surrounded by friends, another surrounded by strangers who dislike them. This is a weird number and often those born within its power go on to great things, as if predestined or driven by the winds of fate. Never underestimate a number-8 person! They have a purpose in life and will fulfill it.

PERSONAL TIPS

Others may think you a little cold at times. You need to express your feelings more. Try telling those you love how you feel; loosen up a bit and let your hair hang down. Everyone knows you're going places, but try to enjoy the journey. You will find that as you grow older you will feel younger. This is because you will learn to let go of all the inner tension you sometimes feel. Hang loose and tune in! And remember, you are loved by your friends.

YOUR PET

Rather shy pets are born under the power of number 8. If you have a dog, cat, or rabbit that hides away from strangers, then it could very well be a number-8 pet. These are very soft creatures that like you to show them a lot of affection. The number-8 dog is not going to be a great guard. They are less aggressive than most other dogs of the same breed and will often just watch as strangers walk right past them. The number-8 cat will like nothing better than a roll around the rug in front of the fire, and it's a real people pet. You can tell a number-8 pet by the way it is always close to its owner or the one it loves best of all. They have lots of pals and are considered to be extremely gentle and loving.

PET TIPS

You must decide what you want from your pet. If it's lots of cuddles and snuggles, then lucky you! Number 8 is up for bags of that. If, on the other hand, you've bought a big breed of dog as a guard and find it hiding under the stairs every time a stranger calls, then you need to train it. Just keep rewarding this pet each time it barks, and pretty soon you will be awake all night as it woofs the house down.
Gentle, kindly, nice, and shy, that's number 8.

THE NUMBER 9

PLANET: Mars
LUCKY DAYS: Tuesday, Thursday
LUCKY COLORS: red, pink
LUCKY JEWELS/STONES: ruby, garnet
LUCKY HEALTH-BRINGING FOOD: onions, garlic, rhubarb

YOU

Very determined and independent people are born under the influence of the number 9. These are the warriors of the world, they will fight without fear and have amazing courage. Often these tough characters will take on more than even they can handle, and this lands our number 9 in plenty big trouble. Frequently foolhardy and reckless, the number-9 boy will often be a rebel, always in at the deep end. The girl number-9 may be the one others long to be like. She will always want to be the centre of attention and just loves it when her friends admire her daring. When it comes to being a fashion queen, then look no further than number 9. These can be very proud people and will not take kindly to criticism, however well meant it may be. The number 9 likes to be looked up to and will stop at nothing to be noticed. You can spot the attention-seeking daredevil number-9 any Saturday night in the casualty ward.

PERSONAL TIPS

Your greatest strength is also your biggest problem: you know no fear. Use this to your advantage by seeking out the very best school courses and the top jobs. Other numbers may be too reserved to apply for the big positions, but not you. Get your mind clear, forget the great I AM, and use your courage to achieve real success.

YOUR PET

The drama queens of the pet world are born under the influence of number 9. These pets want others to look at them day and night. If you hear your cat howling at the Moon outside your bedroom window, well, it's probably a number-9 wanting attention. The number-9 dog is often to be found under your feet. They won't leave you alone — has yours jumped into the bath with you yet? These pets would create a crisis anywhere, just to make you look at them. Often very good-looking, these pets know it, and there is but one thing you can do: applaud.

PET TIPS

Better get to grips nice and early with your number-9 pet. Otherwise it'll be such a show-off, it'll bring the house down for attention. Get your number-9 dog trained at the earliest stage. If you can, get someone who knows about obedience training to help you. These are real fun pets, but it's up to you to establish control.

YOUR STAR-SIGN FRIENDS AND PETS

All of us, people and pets, long to be loved and admired, but sometimes things don't quite work out the way we want them to. Perhaps you and that special boy, girl, cat, dog, or white mouse are just not on the same wavelength. Well, now you can discover for yourself if that dreamboat you are waiting to catch is going to take you on the cruise of a lifetime, or just sail you up the creek.

In Western astrology, each of the twelve signs of the zodiac is ruled by one of the four elements: fire, earth, air, or water. Sometimes opposites attract, but in astrology there is the general rule that like attracts like. There are of course individual exceptions, but some star signs are not usually happy together, and this is deeply connected to the elements. Here are two examples:

LEO (FIRE)　CANCER (WATER)
The fiery, outgoing nature of the Leo sign is dampened by the peaceful, home-loving water sign Cancer. This often creates trouble as Leo will insist on burning bright while Cancer wants a quiet life. The two clash because one sign's needs are directly opposite to the other's.

GEMINI (AIR)　CAPRICORN (EARTH)
The flighty nature of the air sign Gemini is brought thumping down to the ground by the practical earth sign Capricorn. There is bound to be trouble here as Gemini wants to fly off in all directions while Capricorn insists on security and safety.

Look now at each of the four elements and the twelve star signs.

FIRE:
ARIES, LEO, SAGITTARIUS

Fire signs are full of optimism and determination to get things done. Both pets and people will be full of fun and a desire to play and enjoy themselves. Other people are very attracted to these powerful and often outrageous signs.

 ARIES

YOUR FRIENDS

You are a very passionate person who has the power of Mars firing the love lights in your beautiful eyes. Your best bet for a really friendly friend is a lovable Libra or a thoughtful Gemini. Forget the Cancerians, who are too gentle, and the Scorpios, who want the attention that you know should be yours.

YOUR PERFECT PETS

Ruled by Mars, the planet of war, you should have a pet that reflects your attitude and style. Look for an active Gemini pet with a red coat, your lucky color. Dog: red setter. Cat: ginger. Unusual pet: red spider.

 LEO

YOUR FRIENDS

You sparkle and twinkle like the star you really are. Being ruled by the Sun, you are hot stuff, so look to the calming influences of Aquarius and Libra. Dazzle these friends with your brilliant personality. Keep out of the way of Cancer-sign people who want too much of your attention. Scorpios can get lost —you're the star.

YOUR PERFECT PETS

As a Leo you need a top pet that everyone admires. Rare breeds are definitely you. Your pet will have to shine alongside your sunny personality. Interesting Aquarius pets are ideal, and look for light-colored coats or feathers. Dog: British bulldog. Cat: Siamese. Unusual pet: fireflies.

SAGITTARIUS

YOUR FRIENDS

You have a strong power to attract friends. Jupiter makes you think carefully before you pick any pal, but when you decide on your target you usually hit the bullseye. Look to the star signs of Libra and Gemini for true friends who admire your direct approach. Give Pisces and Cancer a miss, they dampen down your fiery nature.

YOUR PERFECT PETS
Your pet must be a real character and have a mind of its own. Clever pets are right for you. Look for quick-learning Gemini pets with dark, shiny coats and lots of personality. Dog: black Labrador. Cat: black. Unusual pet: Vietnamese potbellied pig.

EARTH:
Taurus, Virgo, Capricorn

Earth-sign people and pets seek only true friendship. Generally careful, they know how to make pals and are always faithful. Earth-sign pets are very protective of their owners, and people of their partners; they love with all their hearts. Can be very affectionate when they are with the right one.

 **TAURUS**

YOUR FRIENDS
You are always popular and admired by others. Nothing stops you from stampeding the one that you want into your life. Look to the star signs of Pisces and Cancer for the boy or girl of your dreams. Avoid Aquarius and Libra, these are too flighty for your controlled but passionate nature.

YOUR PERFECT PETS
Big strong pets that will stand by you and protect your home are what you need. You want a friendly pet that knows who's in charge. Look to the sign of Cancer for a guard and a best pal. Dog: German shepherd. Cat: Persian. Unusual pet: bullfrog.

 **VIRGO**

YOUR FRIENDS
Mercury makes you quick to give your heart, though you will give it to only the most beautiful and perfect partner. Seek your boy or girl friends in the star signs of Scorpio and Pisces. Stay away from Gemini

and Sagittarius; your thoughtful, loving ways are lost on them.

YOUR PERFECT PETS

You want a well-trained pet that keeps itself nice and clean. Look for a Scorpio pet, which will remember everything you teach it. The Scorpio pet will be loyal and true to you and guard you with its life. Dog: corgi. Cat: white. Unusual pet: ant farm.

CAPRICORN

YOUR FRIENDS

Selective and particular, you want to be with the right one. Saturn makes you consider every aspect of any would-be boy or girl friend. Others love your sensitive ways. Find true and lasting friendship with a Cancer or Pisces sign. Avoid the signs of Gemini and Aquarius, they are too up in the air for down-to-earth you.

YOUR PERFECT PETS

Your pet will be very close to you. Look at the sign of Pisces for a pet that can tune in to your thoughts. These pets will bring a sense of mystery into your life that will delight you in many ways. Dog: lhasa apso. Cat: Burmese. Unusual pet: fruit bat.

AIR:
Gemini, Libra, Aquarius

These are the romantic lovers that others dream about, but they are flighty types, with more friends and partners than other signs. People and pets born in air signs are charming and often very beautiful.

GEMINI

YOUR FRIENDS

A wonderful sense of fun makes you very popular. Best boy or girl friends are from Leo and Sagittarius, because you can flatter their egos. Those silky words of yours are certain to win you the partner of your choice. But Capricorn and Virgo don't care for your light-hearted approach to love.

YOUR PERFECT PETS

Because you like so much change, you need a very active pet. Birds are going to be near the top of your list, along with chase-about dogs.

Look in the Leo sign for an exciting, dramatic pet. Dog: West Highland white terrier. Cat: tabby. Unusual pet: chameleon.

 LIBRA

YOUR FRIENDS

Venus makes you the one all the others want to trap. Often very beautiful, you will be on the A list for any party. Your charm brings you many boy and girl friends and you enjoy their company. Best partners are from the star signs of Leo and Aries. Stay away from trouble by avoiding Taurus and Capricorn, you're too flighty for them.

YOUR PERFECT PETS

Being a very loving person, you will want a pet that enjoys lots of attention. In the Aries sign you wil find a pet that just loves being cuddled and played with by sweet little you. Dog: Irish wolfhound. Cat: Marmalade moggie. Unusual pet: Venus fly-trap.

AQUARIUS

YOUR FRIENDS

So many friends and so little time, but you will do your best. Never short of pals, you are admired most for your sparkling personality and bright eyes. Best friends come from the strong Leo and Sagittarius signs. Don't get too involved with Taurus or Capricorn, who won't understand your wild and often passionate ways.

YOUR PERFECT PETS

Being so popular, you may need a protective pet. Consider a big strong guard to keep unwanted admirers away. Look to the sign of Leo for a tough but tickle-me pet. Dog: Rough-haired collie. Cat: Siamese. Unusual pet: homing pigeon.

WATER:
Cancer, Scorpio, Pisces

Water-sign pets and people are very faithful and true. These are the trusty companions that one needs to get through tough times. Psychic pets and people are often born in water signs, very influenced by the Moon.

CANCER

YOUR FRIENDS

Ruled by the Moon, you're a sensitive and gentle friend. Others admire your tender, loving ways and you are always good company. You will seek true and constant companions. Best boy or girl friends come from the Taurus and Capricorn signs. Avoid the big show-off sign of Leo and stay away from Aries.

YOUR PERFECT PETS

Being so gentle and home-loving, you will be happiest with a pet that shares your values. Look in the sign of Capricorn for your perfect pet, one that will be contented at home and a good guard. Dog: white poodle. Cat: black. Unusual pet: fiddler crab.

SCORPIO

YOUR FRIENDS

Your powerful personality means you are in great demand. Would-be pals are always seeking you out — do you hypnotize them? Find your best boy or girl friends in the signs of Virgo and Capricorn; they just adore your presence. Beware of getting too close to Leo and Aries signs, they insist on being the centre of attention and dislike your popularity.

YOUR PERFECT PETS

Something out of the ordinary is what you look for in a pet. You expect your pet to be very clever and should always seek an intelligent breed. Look to the sign of Virgo to find your pet pal. Dog: Border collie. Cat: Manx. Unusual pet: piranha fish.

 # PISCES

YOUR FRIENDS

Others enjoy your company and think you're a wonderful talker. Often the centre of attention, you can spot the one you want across any crowded room. Your best boy or girl friends are found in Taurus and Virgo. Keep out of the way of Leo and Sagittarius.

YOUR PERFECT PETS

You want a pet that returns your trust and love. A friendly pet that welcomes you home with a tail wag and a show of affection is your idea of a pal. Look in the sign of Taurus for a loyal, loving pet Dog: cocker spaniel. Cat: tortoiseshell. Unusual pet: buffalo.

THE TWELVE HOUSES

Use this section in conjunction with the Astro-Dowsing Chart to discover the influence of the planets in relation to yourself and your pet. Remember that these are outlines, and you must use your own judgement. Look carefully at the explanations given, think about them and, using your common sense, interpret them. It's no good blaming Mercury if you fall asleep in class — try going to bed earlier.

THE 12 HOUSES

In Western astrology, the birth chart is divided into sections called houses. Each house has a specific meaning and it is the position of the planets in these houses at the time of birth that enables the astrologer to predict the influences affecting any pet's or person's future.

The following is a list of the twelve houses and their areas of influence. How the planets in these houses affect you and your pet will be explained in the following section.

THE 1ST HOUSE: the self, you or your pet

The first house is also called **the ascendant** and is the sign rising in any chart. This is the house of you as an individual, the point from which you progress. Any planet in this house has a powerful effect upon the character. How you or your pet are seen by others is ruled by this house. Powerful planets in this house exert a lot of force. Self-awareness and personal outlooks on life are formed in this important house.

If your pet is to be a prizewinner, look here for signs of success.

THE 2ND HOUSE:
material possessions and ownership

Money, all forms of ownership, and personal possessions are influenced by this house. Those with important planets here are going to be wealthy and prosperous in life. This is the house of worldly goods and the way in which you acquire them. In this house you will find your material future. Be it good or bad fortune, within the boundaries of the 2nd house it waits.

Pets with planet power here will have all the comforts any creature could desire.

THE 3RD HOUSE:
the mind, thoughts and communication

Logical thought, clear thinking, and control of the emotions are here. The deep thinkers who devise great schemes will have the planets of power here in their charts. Whoever seeks to be a broadcaster or other communicator should look within this house. The practical mind, the planner, the creator, the architect who would build a bridge to the stars are within this strange and very controlled house of the mind.

Pets empowered by the planets in this house will be very clever. They can communicate their needs to their owners. Look here for the really quick learners.

THE 4TH HOUSE:
home, where you and your pet live

The place we call home is here in this house. Each one of us, pet and person, has a special little area on Earth that we identify as being our place. Many think that this is where they were born, but this is not so. We create our homes by our thoughts and deeds. You are the master of your destiny, and the power of the planets in this house will help you decide if you will call a castle in Spain home, or an apartment on 42nd Street, New York. There's no place like home, so click your heels and look out for Munchkins.

Pets with a powerful planet here will have the very best sleeping quarters in the home.

THE 5TH HOUSE:
happiness, joy, popularity

If you are seeking a life creating happiness and living each day to the full, you must look here in the 5th house. The planets in this house of fun can empower you and your pet to bring a sense of joy and wonderment to the rest of the world. Here the creative geniuses who dazzle others with their words and music find their fortune. Those who seek to entertain, especially on the stage, screen, or radio, should seek the power of the planets within this house. The most popular people are empowered here.   The pet with plenty of planet power here will always be smothered with love.

THE 6TH HOUSE: work, duty, service

The house of hard work and the ability to succeed. You should look within for the power to further the ideas you had in the 5th house. There can be no great success without endeavour, and to reach your goal you will need to apply yourself. To use your gifts, whatsoever they may be, you must work hard developing them.

Look here for pets that have work to do: guide dogs, sheep dogs, farm dogs. Any pet that would be a good therapy animal will have planets empowering this house.

THE 7TH HOUSE:
friends, relationships, lovelife

Those seeking knowledge of their future friends and relationships should look for the power of the planets here. This is the house of love, marriage, and partnership. Those who find this house empowered by the strongest planets will be blessed with the love of many and the admiration of all. Within this house is the response to all that we do or have done. To learn how friends see you, enter this house and look around. Remember, love waits for all who seek it.

Your pet with powerful planets here will have more pals than any other animal in town. If you are thinking of mating your pet, seek the answer here.

THE 8TH HOUSE:
money and partnerships, changes

Unlike the 2nd house, the 8th house contains the money and material goods you or your pet may receive through others. Search here for the fortune you expect to inherit from rich Uncle Bert. Look within this house for a special partnership or marriage that brings great wealth. Here is change and progression through joint enterprise or by gift from one to another. Powerful planets in this house bring both riches and new beginnings. Keep a pure heart and be careful what you look for here you may just find it.

Pets that receive lots of presents are empowered in this house of unexpected gifts.

THE 9TH HOUSE:
social systems, learning

Society has certain systems that help maintain the status quo. These obviously vary from country to country as each nation has its own culture. The 9th is the house of rules and belief systems. The law, religion, and education are to be found here. Those strongly empowered by planets in this house may shape the spiritual thinking of their culture by new teachings. The wise ones find here the strength to dream.

Pets that follow the rules of the home have powerful planets in this house of order.

THE 10TH HOUSE:
honor, reputation, career

You will create your career, your life's work and reputation in this house, the 10th. Here are the great ones whose names live on forever in the folklore of our countries. With strong planets in this house, you will be a determined and successful player in the game of life. You should look within this house if you would change the world, for those empowered here can do just that.

Pets with powerful planets in this house will be unstoppable guards and loyal friends.

THE 11TH HOUSE:
teamwork, togetherness

Creating any major or lasting change really needs a group effort. No one person can ever hope to do everything on their own. Here in this house you should seek the power of the planets to strengthen teamwork. Together with other like-minded individuals you can achieve your goals, whatever they may be. Look here for creative partnerships. If the planets in this house are strong, nothing and no one will stop your team.

Pets that are sociable and happy in groups have powerful planets here.

THE 12TH HOUSE:
spirituality, the psychic

Look here for mystical, almost magical influence. With strong planets in this house, you and your pet may be very psychic. There is great depth of understanding here in the 12th and final house. Seek here if you would find the ultimate answer to your questions. The last house is, however, not the finish, it is both the end and the beginning. Those empowered here will see that for they have a sixth sense that opens the door into the dimensions beyond.

There is peace, truth, and wisdom here, just look and you shall find.

Pets with strong planets in this house seem almost able to read your mind.

THE PLANETS

Each of the twelve houses is only as strong as the planets that empower it. There are degrees of influence, and certain planets in certain houses are believed to create very powerful vibrations that transmit to this world and all within it. To find out where the planets in your own or your pet's chart are, refer to the section on astro-dowsing.

The following is an introduction to the planets and the nature of the power they exert upon each of the twelve houses.

THE SUN

This planet is the centre of existence in our great and wonderful solar system. In astrology, the Sun brings the power and creative energy you need to achieve your full potential.

The 1st House
YOU

Great power to lead others. Imaginative and creative. Clear thinking. Determined and forceful. Energetic and very active. Healthy and strong. Ambitious. Brave.

YOUR PET

Proud, rather showy. Catwalk cat or dog-show dog. Big for breed. Great guard. Tough.

The 2nd House
YOU

Learning lessons of responsible ownership and to use your money for the benefit of others. Beware of being too flashy. Money often wasted on folly. Big-heads be warned, cool it!

YOUR PET

Popular and pretty. Strong character. Lucky and luxurious life.

The 3rd House
YOU

Intellectual and clever. Scientific mind power enhanced. Exploring new areas. Travel is well aspected. Very close to family and relatives. Good communicator. Studious.

YOUR PET

Very quick to learn. Plays tricks. Often missing or off exploring. Garden digger.

The 4th House
YOU

Interested in family tree and ancestors. You create a secure and smart, if rather flashy, home. Early struggles lead to great success. Dominant personality.

YOUR PET

Clean and well groomed. Lovely coat. Easy to house-train. Careful eater, not messy.

The 5th House

YOU

You like to be noticed and seek constant attention. Can be too self-confident. Great lover. Happy, with many friends who bask in your sunshine. Pleasure seeker.

YOUR PET

Happy and cuddly. A real softy.

The 6th House

YOU

Good worker. Need a lot of praise. Sometimes very demanding of others working with you. You set high standards. May suffer from ill health at work. Very dignified and proud.

YOUR PET

Really strong and big for breed. Great guard. Determined and never gives in.

The 7th House

YOU

Forceful lover who can dominate any relationship. Seen as self-confident and very able, you attract much admiration. Loyal and loving. Good friend or marriage partner.

YOUR PET

Most chased-after pet on the block. Friendly and lovable. Loyal and home-loving.

The 8th House

YOU

Determined in your efforts. Inheritance of wealth highly likely. Divorce from partner. Lawsuits and court cases possible. Overspending a danger here. Chance-taking is very risky!

YOUR PET

Risk-taking but very lucky. Great Climper. Road runner and car chaser. Danger pet!

The 9th House

YOU

Interested in other cultures and beliefs. Can be very religious. The study of law or religion is empowered. Will travel widely. Can be rather uptight about love and partners.

YOUR PET

Comes when you call. Obedient and easy to teach. Stands by your side loyally.

The 10th House

YOU

Very ambitious. A hard worker, you aim for the top and will not accept failure. A winner. Noble and dignified. You tend to be rather too proud.

YOUR PET

The greatest guard. Tougher than tough. The bravest pet in town. Fearless and bold.

The 11th House

YOU

Lots of good friends. Well thought of and loved by others. A good team player. Will lead any group with friendly dignity. Very smart operator. Can be selfish at times.

YOUR PET

Everybody's favorite pet. Very popular with other animals. Plays well with others. Gentle.

The 12th House

YOU

Can be a loner or book worm. Search for enlightenment never ends. Helping others is strongly aspected. You may be very psychic with mystical powers.

Moon-struck. Spooky cat or storm-howling dog. Mysterious and mystical.

THE MOON

In astrology, the Moon represents sensitivity and emotional response to situations in life. It is believed to be a major influence on the way we relate to others.

The 1st House
YOU
Moody and temperamental. Lack of direction. Too easily influenced by others. You may be given to food fads or overeating. Highly emotional. Psychic powers. Need for praise. Very self-conscious.

YOUR PET
Moon-struck. A greedy eater. Overweight. Rather lazy. A snoozer and snorer.

The 2nd House
YOU
Searching for security. Good at business dealings. Money comes through personal efforts. You save every spare penny. Skilled in home management.

YOUR PET
Luxury lifestyle. Comfortable cat or domesticated dog. Secure and contented.

The 3rd House
YOU
Imaginative. Bit of a daydreamer. Many moves of home. Can become involved in trivial pursuits. Lacking in logic. With guidance can succeed with the most fantastic ideas.

YOUR PET
Curiosity kills these cats and dogs. Will sniff at everything, burrow into bags. A wanderer.

The 4th House
YOU
Strong need to feel loved. Close to parents, especially mother. Great cook. Good homemaker. Financial security in later life. Family ties are extra important. Gentle and kind.

YOUR PET
Follows you everywhere. Very loving and gentle. Can be a fussy eater.

The 5th House
YOU
Highly active imagination brings you very different kinds of friends. Lots of children in your life. Very romantic ideas about your partner. Family may interfere in your lovelife.

YOUR PET
Good for breeding. Very affectionate and loyal. Loves all others in the home. A popular pet.

The 6th House
YOU
A real pet lover. Good at organizing diets and menus. Ideal as a chef or restaurant manager. Lot of job changes. Emotional outbursts at work place. Imaginary illnesses affect work.

YOUR PET
Fussy eater. Seems a little less strong than other pets. Moody at times. Friendly.

The 7th House
YOU
You will seek out a strong marriage partner to lean on in time of trouble. You are kindly and loving, loyal and true to your lover. Can become dependent on love of partner.

YOUR PET
Sits on your knee or clings close to you all the time. Very loving and loyal.

The 8th House
YOU
Psychic powers lead you to a family fortune. Marriage may bring money from inheritance. You are likely to be beautiful. Usually get your way in partnerships. Property affairs are well aspected.

YOUR PET
Very clever. Snuggles up to whoever has the treats. Lovely-looking and cute.

The 9th House
YOU
Early religious influences bring respect for moral standards. Strict parents that have tough house rules. Ruled by emotion but will reluctantly conform. Steady learner.

YOUR PET
Easy to train. Keeps all the rules of the house. Can be a very good guard. Loyal and true.

The 10th House
YOU
Parents can be too ambitious for you to succeed. Careers in the public eye are a good choice. Beware of the influence of a powerful lady. You need to achieve great things.

YOUR PET
Brave guard. Likes to be looked at, can be rather proud. A show-off.

The 11th House
YOU
Many friends that you will work with, at home. Lots of different work opportunities. You are good in a team but may be moody at times. Many changes but you are never alone.

YOUR PET
Loves being with other pets. Other creatures love it. Can be a little selfish at times.

The 12th House
YOU
Very sensitive, perhaps a little shy. Psychic studies are powerfully aspected. Emotions can be too strong to control. Great powers of assessment. Beware of being too moody.

YOUR PET
Sulky. This pet wants all its own way. Can be quite telepathic or psychic.

JUPITER
In astrology Jupiter is linked to spiritual and religious beliefs. Thoughts of higher things, the meaning of life and our real purpose on Earth, are influenced by Jupiter. This is the planet of personal responsibility, of good and bad fortune.

The 1st House
YOU
Bright and breezy personality. Always looking for the best in others. Seen as a deep thinker. Very moral and upright. Full of great promise. Strong beliefs. A leader of others.

YOUR PET
Happy as the day is long. Deeply loving and stands by you. Playful and fun.

The 2nd House
YOU
Good luck for you in property dealing. Money comes through your business skills. Can be too free with money. Beware of taking major risks — think things through. You will travel abroad.

YOUR PET
Loses its toys all the time. Loves playing, but very careless and carefree.

The 3rd House
YOU
You write your thoughts down, probably keep a diary. Logical and always aware of all the options. Strong speaker with good command of facts. Social thinker. Culture vulture.

YOUR PET
Travel-happy. Loves trips out into the country. Tendency to disappear.

The 4th House
YOU
Happy and usually secure home life. Prosperous parents. Education leads to important houses and homes. Well-connected family. Surrounded by relatives, particularly older relations.

YOUR PET
Often two pets from same parents live together. Easy to get along with. Clean and tidy.

The 5th House
YOU
Joy through romance with a rich person. Sport brings great pleasure. Playing team games makes you very popular. Educational achievements create great opportunities.

YOUR PET
Very active, this pet will run you into the ground. Nonstop game-player. A good buddy.

The 6th House
YOU
Practical. You may become an architect or a civil engineer. You also have good healing gifts, and the desire and ability to help others. Medical skills come naturally. Popular. Pleasing personality at work.

YOUR PET
A kindly pet that seems to care for other animals. Very gentle but can be a determined guard.

The 7th House
YOU
Good luck and money, often through marriage. Good life partner, loyal and true. Gentle and loving, honest and friendly. Admired by others, who see you as very spiritual.

YOUR PET
What you see is what you get. This character wears its heart on its collar.

The 8th House
YOU
Money and property may be inherited. Your career may involve partnership in a large concern, perhaps an accountancy firm. Taxation and related matters are present. Often wealthy.

YOUR PET
Very sensitive, may seem to have telepathic powers. Loves you a lot.

The 9th House
YOU
Often involved in religious movements. A keen student, you will achieve top grades. You may undertake long journeys to study other cultures. Interest in the law is well aspected.

YOUR PET
Fast-learning, this pet quickly masters new tricks. Sticks by the rules of the house.

The 10th House
YOU
Very ambitious. High achievement in the professions may be yours. Honest and very reliable. Politically aware. You wear all the right clothes. You will have money and even great wealth.

YOUR PET
Will to win. Very determined, gets what it wants. Brave guard.

The 11th House
YOU
Great success within groups. Often involved in charity work. Well respected and liked. Educational teamwork well aspected. Good at getting others together for a project.

YOUR PET
Good worker. Loves playing together with other pets. Unselfish, will share everything.

The 12th House
YOU
Mystical and often psychic. Sympathetic, generous and gentle. Great understanding of others' needs. Healing powers. Charity work is well aspected. May live on Fantasy Island.

YOUR PET
Helps others and befriends weaker pets. A real therapy pet. Can be a dreamer.

URANUS

In astrology Uranus is believed to be the planet of personal action. It channels the force that makes you do things. The reasoning behind your deeds is influenced by Uranus. How you as an individual approach situations and life chances is subject to this planet of motivation.

The 1st House
YOU
Out of the ordinary. Others see you as a bit different, even weird or spooky. You switch opinion from one extreme to another. Highly intelligent with lots of strange ideas. Odd friends.

YOUR PET
This pet has some strange attitudes. It won't do what's expected of it. Bizarre and unpredictable.

The 2nd House
YOU
A risk-taker, you often lose money. You will have odd ways of gaining income. Trouble over money you owe. Perhaps a gambler, you can make money quickly, then lose it. Cash through strange inventions.

YOUR PET
A roving pet that likes to take chances. Chases over the fields and gets lost. Crazy creature.

The 3rd House
YOU
Ideas and original thoughts flood your mind. You leap from one impossible project to another. Totally impractical. Confused and confusing. As a speaker, you are exciting and excitable.

YOUR PET
No one knows what this pet will do next. Life with this creature is never dull.

The 4th House
YOU
Weird groups and friends come to your home to meet. Your parents are out of the ordinary. Lots of strange equipment around you. Odd home, and you will live in many different houses.

YOUR PET
Sleeps in the garden or anywhere odd. Takes many strange things into its bed.

The 5th House
YOU
Lots of love affairs. You hate being tied down with just one partner. Happiness found through membership of some artistic group. Odd friends and weird lovers. You're a pleasure seeker.

YOUR PET
Probably a stray pet that found you. It will bring home other odd or lost pets. Luxurious and wants lots of love.

The 6th House
YOU
Technical and inventive. Original and creative worker. Good with others to help develop new ideas. Best working with freedom to make decisions. Soon bored. Bad temper.

YOUR PET
Always finds a new way home. Loves long walks into strange places. Explores and gets lost.

The 7th House
YOU
You will fall in love with a very weird person. Quickly bored within one relationship, you change your lovers like socks. People often disappoint you. Friends see you as moody.

YOUR PET
Can't make its mind up. One minute playful, next minute not interested. Moody.

The 8th House
YOU
Rapid change in fortune, often by inheriting vast amounts of money. You may experience some serious loss of money. You will understand the meaning of friendship, life, and spirituality.

YOUR PET
Lucky pet that get lots of attention. Prizewinner. Many friends. Intelligent.

The 9th House
YOU
You enjoy searching for New Age answers. Astrology is one of your interests. Education will involve you in highly technical computer systems. Mysterious countries await you.

YOUR PET
Unusual. Has extraordinary tastes — this pet may be a cat that likes bones or a dog that eats fish.

The 10th House
YOU
Way out and off the wall. A totally unique person, you may change the world but not your socks. Possibly a genius. Quick rise to fame and fortune: up like a rocket, down like the stick.

YOUR PET
Does what it wants. Looks at you as if you're crazy, or ignores you. Unique.

The 11th House
YOU
Likely to become involved in group work with a scientific team. Membership of some strange and mysterious movement. Sometimes too selfish. Odd and unusual friends. Spiritual.

YOUR PET
A loner, happiest with just you for company. Can be a little aggressive.

The 12th House
YOU
Mystical influences are all around you. Meditation and study of the ancient arts. Spiritual, you may even be very psychic. Beware: do not dabble in the unknown, seek guidance.

Telepathic, reads your mind. Mystery pets that seem to appear from nowhere have Uranus in the 12 house. Spooky.

MERCURY

In astrology the planet Mercury stands for communication. Mercury is the planet of thought and mind power linked to the ability to develop imaginative ideas.

The 1st House
YOU
Intelligent and organized. Clear thinker who never misses a trick. Writing is well aspected. Great ability to express thoughts. Others see you as a future big success. You can do it!

YOUR PET
Smartest pet in town. Knows all the house rules and how to break them.

The 2nd House
YOU
Great methods of moneymaking bring you many of life's glittering prizes. Use your mind to create wealth, it is there for you. You are a high achiever whom others look up to. Riches galore.

YOUR PET
Quick as quicksilver, intelligent. Not backward in coming forward.

The 3rd House
YOU
Talent for writing and broadcasting. You write long letters and are always on the phone or online. Very creative and capable of communicating ideas. Stick to the truth!

YOUR PET
This pet could teach you a few tricks. Smart. Once told, never forgotten.

The 4th House
YOU
May work from home. Often parents are wealthy. Constantly on the move. May live in foreign countries. Home is where the office is. Often surrounded with books and papers.

YOUR PET
Sleeping box full of toys. Will sleep wherever the playthings are. Happy-go-lucky.

The 5th House
YOU
Artistic, perhaps a writer. Often gifted musically, with lots of like-minded, arty friends. Interested in education of the young. Might become a teacher of art or drama. Likely member of a poetry group.

YOUR PET
Makes friends easily. A happy creature, this pet likes a stroke from all, even total strangers.

The 6th House
YOU
Always smart and tidy. Very neat worker with everything in its place. You follow the rules. Efficient, you get the job done. You dislike messy work and are too critical. Brainy and bright.

YOUR PET
Clean and always well groomed. Ideal therapy pet. Well disciplined. Clever and controlled

The 7th House
YOU
You tend to examine all the options before acting. Rather cool at first in any love match, but later WOW! You have close friendships but not too many Aloof. Clever.

YOUR PET
Wins both hearts and prizes. Very gentle. Seems to pick its pals with great care.

The 8th House
YOU
Good chance of inheriting money. Many strange and often spooky friends. You're likely to travel, and this may be connected to older relations. Very careful with money. Secretive. Nervous.

YOUR PET
Off chasing moonbeams. A creature of the night. Unexpected journeys. Goes missing.

The 9th House
YOU
High achiever at school. Your mind is like a computer, every piece of information in place. Member of the top clubs. Often religious. Must understand how things work.

YOUR PET
Rather difficult to understand. Very quick to learn games, then refuses to play. Odd creature.

The 10th House
YOU
A potential professor. Very ambitious in the field of higher education. Use your knowledge and educational qualifications to earn lots of money in a high-status job. You are deliberate, a planner.

YOUR PET
Too smart to fight. Thoughtful and always up to new tricks. This pet will surprise you.

The 11th House
YOU
Member of a self-help group. Good team player, you bring ideas and organizational skills to team activities. Very gentle and understanding of others' needs. Fair-minded. Could become a teacher.

YOUR PET
The dog at front of the pack. The loudest cat in the choir. This pet thinks we are all pals together.

The 12th House
YOU
Very imaginative. Psychic powers. Sometimes rather shy. Creative writer. Feelings and past experiences form the basis for your decisions. Not logical at times. Early learning problems.

YOUR PET
Difficult to train when young. Runs off and hides.Loves you to bits, then gets lost. Weird.

VENUS

In astrology the planet of love and romance is Venus. Social skills and the way we relate to others are influenced. The kind of people we meet, marry, and live with are linked to Venus.

The 1st House
YOU
Physically beautiful. Attractive to members of the opposite sex. Many friends. Contented, happy childhood. Popular with others. Artistic. Well dressed. Charming. Musical. Lucky!

YOUR PET
Glamour puss or swanky dog. Great fun to play with. Lovely coat. Shining eyes. Friendly.

The 2nd House
YOU
Wealth and prosperity. You may have, or acquire, lots of fabulous possessions: jewels and gold, wonderful paintings and other artistic treasures. Marvellous houses. Extravagant lifestyle. Hey, big spender!

YOUR PET
Simply the best collar in town. Comfortable life of luxury. "Treat me now!"

The 3rd House
YOU
Artistically gifted. Perhaps a poet or painter, you have the ability to communicate beautiful ideas through your work, or capture emotions in words. You are romantic and a sweet talker.

YOUR PET
Dreamy eyes. Looks at you with love. Rolls over to be tickled. Gentle and loving.

The 4th House
YOU
Home-loving. You enjoy giving parties at home, and always have lots of friends round the house. You have loving, kind parents. You are likely to be a good gardener and you love having beautiful things in the home. Happy.

YOUR PET
Outside, racing round the garden or climbing a tree. Very territorial, a good guard.

The 5th House
YOU
Many romantic affairs of the heart. Very popular with others, especially of the opposite sex. Talented stage performer whom others love to watch. Entertainer. Full of happiness.

YOUR PET
Always off with the gang or having its pet pals pop round.

The 6th House
YOU
Fashion- and design-conscious. Very artistic, you will create many beautiful things. Romantic meetings at work or school. You like to work hard, but only in nice, clean places.

YOUR PET
Good worker, if a dog. Loving and friendly, if a cat. This pet knows who loves it. Clever.

The 7th House
YOU
Very popular, others like being with you. Romantic marriage, often at an early age. Considerate and kind. Many seek you for your good looks. Lots of loving friends.

YOUR PET
Other animals are attracted to this pet. Great fun but often off playing with pals.

The 8th House
YOU
Wealth through marriage. Inheritance of riches. Can be too sexy. Rather emotional with outbursts and crying crocodile tears. Jealous of others. Friendship to seek personal gain.

YOUR PET
Attention seeker. Can be greedy. Pushy pet. "I like me, who do you like?" attitude.

The 9th House
YOU
Travel involved with research and learning. Education often centers on art. Can be very religious, especially linked to obscure beliefs. Love of culture and history. Artistic.

YOUR PET
Likes lots of walks and exercise. Knows the area it lives in really well. Quick to learn.

The 10th House
YOU
Success in work through romance. Very well liked at school and work. Others admire your artistic creations. The theatre and performing arts are highlighted. Social success.

YOUR PET
Would make a good guide dog (unless it's a cat). Very friendly and ideal companion. A good therapy animal.

The 11th House
YOU
Pop-group membership possible, or membership of some artistic circle. You work well with most teams and have many musical friends. Others respect your creative talents, perhaps as a poet or painter.

YOUR PET
Happiest when in a home with other pets. A dog that likes cats, or a cat that likes everyone.

The 12th House
YOU
Secret love affairs. Forever searching for the love of your life. May be rather shy. Very gentle and kind to others. A deep thinker, you like to meditate alone. You may be an inspired artist.

YOUR PET
Much given to sitting alone and dreaming. Star-gazing and moon-struck. Gentle and kindly.

NEPTUNE

In astrology Neptune is believed to influence the creative and the artistic. Dreams and visions of the future are empowered by this planet of mystery and imagination.

The 1st House
YOU
Others see you as mysterious and interesting. You will have powerful artistic gifts — as a poet, painter, or musician — and psychic powers. Beware of being too trusting. Never mess with magic.

YOUR PET
Strong personality. Hypnotic eyes. Beautiful and mysterious.

The 2nd House
YOU
Can make a lot of money through original ideas. Mystery may surround you and your possessions. Beware of overspending. Your personal property is often magnificent.

YOUR PET
Amazingly lucky, this pet receives all sorts of presents. Very proud and noble.

The 3rd House
YOU
Ideas and visions from another dimension. Very good speaker on TV and radio. Great communicator of deep thoughts. A dreamer. You may take up writing or broadcasting under other names.

YOUR PET
Understanding, seems to know how you're feeling. Very gentle and cuddly.

The 4th House
YOU
Parents with mysterious powers. You will probably live near water, perhaps the sea. You bring strangers into your home. There are deep family secrets. Trouble with parents.

YOUR PET
Disruptive, often noisy. If a dog, it barks; if a cat, may collect dead birds.

The 5th House
YOU
The theatre brings you happiness. You have many friendships that you keep to yourself. You are popular with artistic groups. Romance brings joy, but beware of being too hungry to be loved.

YOUR PET
Must have attention all the time. Can be sulky and moody if left alone for periods.

The 6th House
YOU
Very efficient and determined worker. Caring for others is well aspected. With your strange ability to tune in to pets, you may become involved in the care of animals. Spiritual.

YOUR PET
Psychic, able to help you through mystical means. A paranormal pet.

The 7th House
YOU
Romantic and very loving, you will be a gentle and kind lover. You will have a strong psychic bond with your partner. You will have artistic friends. Beware of involvement with legal matters and the courts.

YOUR PET
In tune with you and all within the home. This is a one-owner pet that will just love you to bits.

The 8th House
YOU
Strange and often disturbing influences surround your involvement in others' affairs. Beware of being tricked or trying to trick others. If possible, avoid working partnerships.

YOUR PET
Tricky pets that know all the dodges. Can be rather sneaky in trying to get their own way.

The 9th House
YOU
Never get involved in cults. You will be seeking spiritual enlightenment, so ignore the big-heads who tell lies. Concentrate on your formal education. Beware of foolish false praise.

YOUR PET
Easy to lead astray. Off up the road and into all sorts of trouble.

The 10th House
YOU
Your professional life will be out of the ordinary. Perhaps you'll become an actor, a rock musician, an astrologer, or a psychic. Avoid the temptation to cheat your way to the top. Your parents may have a weird influence.

YOUR PET
Everyone notices this outrageous show-off. Can be up to tricks if you don't watch it.

The 11th House
YOU
Genuine and honest with your work team. Others look to you for guidance. You may join some strange, mysterious movement — be careful! Beware of secret enemies and deceptions.

YOUR PET
Other pets seek this one out as a friend. It will often have its toys pinched by these friends.

The 12th House
YOU
You will gain knowledge from the fourth, unseen, dimension. Mystical psychic powers. Beware of dabbling in the occult. Be spiritual. You have a powerful, sensitive nature.

YOUR PET
Telepathic and psychic. Likes to stare at the stars. Spooky!

SATURN

In astrology Saturn is seen as the planet of self-discipline. With this planet in an important house, you will be empowered to progress and build a meaningful life. This is the planet of personal responsibility. Time to grow up.

The 1st House
YOU
Others see you as very serious. You are logical and determined. You may have hard times when young, but that makes you tough. Responsible and admired. Often in charge. Obstacles.

YOUR PET
A tough guy, ready for action, will fight anyone. A great guard, but watch it!   (Unless it's a guinea pig.)

The 2nd House
YOU
An extra-hard worker, you really succeed. The way you save your money, you'll end up with a big bank account. Property deals are well aspected. Good introductions through family. You have the ability to build up wealth.

YOUR PET
A selfish pet that won't share its toys. Hoards treats.

The 3rd House
YOU
You're a practical thinker who weighs all the odds carefully. A slow speaker, you consider each word. Tend to worry over nothing. Good with mathematical problems. You dislike traveling.

YOUR PET
Suffers from travel sickness, and will run a mile rather than get in a car. Never forgets a thing.

The 4th House
YOU
You have parents that lay down the law. Hard work will be required to get a nice home. You need to escape to another area. There'll be struggles and strife as you make your own life. You must do your own thing.

YOUR PET
"Who pinched my toys?" look. Rather sad-eyed and sorrowful, hard done by.

The 5th House
YOU
You will achieve happiness through art, especially music, and probably working within the world of entertainment. Your life is full of new challenges, each day is different.   You are very creative, popular, and a bit strange.

YOUR PET
Will try anything once. Knows no barriers. Given to running off to have an adventure.

The 6th House
YOU
Efficient and serious-minded, you're a hard worker. You may find yourself working in a very specialized field like scientific research. Logical, careful, and capable, you will be well respected and quickly promoted.

YOUR PET
Plods along with a "nothing bothers me" attitude. Steady and reliable, makes a good working pet.

The 7th House
YOU
Marriage to an older person. You will always be fair and true in love. You take full share of responsibility in any relationship. May want to organize others. Will keep your word.

YOUR PET
Bossy, will push others out of their way. "I'm in charge here" attitude. Stares you out.

The 8th House
YOU
You're good at managing other people's money and property. Lack of money creates the need to form partnership. You are very responsible and must maintain the highest standards.

YOUR PET
Eats other pets' food. Greedy, always hungry. Very active.

The 9th House
YOU
Formal education and achievement of good exam results. Progress through religious connections. Legal studies well aspected. Study in other lands. High moral standards.

YOUR PET
Wouldn't harm a fly. Quiet and thoughtful. Very gentle. Needs lots of attention.

The 10th House
YOU
A power seeker, you are strong-minded, with no inhibitions. Beware of being too determined. Great things can be achieved, but there will be obstacles. You may be involved in some disgrace.

YOUR PET
Thought bubbles: "Get out of my way." "Look at me, I'm wonderful!"

The 11th House
YOU
You will be helped by powerful friends. Working in a team with older, more experienced people brings success. Fair-minded, you will divide benefits equally. Joint enterprises.

YOUR PET
Shares everything. Good-tempered and playful. Many friends.

The 12th House
YOU
Thinking and studying alone makes you too self-centered. Others may reject your well-thought-out plans. By helping others you will help yourself. A loner. You must be practical.

YOUR PET
"Leave me alone" attitude. Can be rather moody. Stares into thin air and thinks too much.

MARS
In astrology Mars is seen as the planet of action and power. The influence of Mars brings energy and the ability to achieve goals. Those seeking fame and glory must have Mars empowering one of their important houses.

The 1st House
YOU
Strong and muscular. Self-motivated. Quick temper. You can be a show-off with a high opinion of yourself. Potential for high achievement as a dynamic leader. Intolerant.

YOUR PET
Big and powerful for breed. Fearless guard. An active, risk-taking pet that runs everywhere.

The 2nd House
YOU
A good worker who'll earn lots of money. You're generous, often too much so, but determined to achieve wealth. Although you always aim to have the best, you can be too quick to spend on foolish things.

YOUR PET
Good working pet — farm dog or guard. Brave, will protect its property and yours. This does not apply to goldfish.

The 3rd House
YOU
A quick thinker, rather impulsive. Thoughtless remarks can be insulting to others. Often angry Sure of yourself. You have journalistic skills, are a determined communicator and a powerful speaker.

YOUR PET
Aggressive, takes what it wants. Rather fierce guard. A big, hungry pet.

The 4th House
YOU
DIY crazy, always decorating. You're the king or queen of your own personal castle. Never quite satisfied with your house, you'll frequently move to better property. The Big Boss is here!

YOUR PET
Pinches your bed. Rather pushy and determined. Shoves other pets out of the way.

The 5th House
YOU
Very passionate and popular with others, especially of the opposite sex. Can be jealous of some people. Others find you intelligent and fun to be with, though rather bossy at times.

YOUR PET
Rough, tough game-player. Likes to be outdoors and run with the pack. A hunter.

The 6th House
YOU
A strong and skillful worker, gifted with mechanical ability. Capable and careful. Practical. Tendency to work too hard. High expectations of yourself and others. Efficient.

YOUR PET
Learns quickly. Good working pet, though as a guard rather too ready to fight. Loyal.

The 7th House
YOU
Very sexy. Likely to be involved with more than one partner at a time. Often in trouble with lovers. Impulsive changes. Many friends, but you tend to make enemies out of friends.

YOUR PET
Always in fights. Could cause a riot in a monastery. Likes other pets — for dinner.

The 8th House
YOU
Joint financial ventures well aspected. You get things done and you'll earn money. There is a possibility of your involvement in court cases or other battles. One or more of your friendships will be linked to psychic matters. You tend to be aggressive.

YOUR PET
Self-protective. Jealous guard of its property. Fearless fighter and very strong.

The 9th House
YOU
Inspired leader. Very moral, with good understanding of right and wrong. You will travel abroad, and this will be linked to religion. Great adventures await. A revolutionary. Strong in your beliefs.

YOUR PET
Very ordered, regular as clockwork. Can be too demanding if you're late.

The 10th House
YOU
Fame and glory, or possibly infamy, await you. You are a high achiever with a strong urge to reach the top, and may take a no-holds-barred attitude — you fight to win. A powerful personality.

YOUR PET
The one pet everyone has heard of. The best guard, fighter, scratcher in town. Grrrrrrr!

The 11th House
YOU
Good team player but very determined to win at all costs. Inventive and creative, you will find a way to make your group the tops. Can be very critical of failure. Quarrelsome.

YOUR PET
"I'll have it my way, or else!" attitude. The boss. Other pets have to accept second place.

The 12th House
YOU
Good at keeping secrets. You think deep thoughts, alone. Politically minded. Capable of making great plans. May have unseen enemies. Beware of involvement with extreme groups.

YOUR PET
Rather bad-tempered. One minute fine and dandy, next growling and scratching.

PLUTO
In astrology Pluto is the planet of change, for good or evil. Your power to create new opportunities and move forward in life is influenced by the position of Pluto in your chart.

The 1st House
YOU
Strong willpower. Often difficult times during early years, and this makes you determined. Some see you as deep and mysterious. Highly original outlook on life. Hypnotic eyes.

YOUR PET
A foundling, or a pet that was hurt when young. Spooky eyes. A hypno-pet.

The 2nd House
YOU
Many original ways of making money. You will want to own everything — be rational! Good insight into hidden opportunities. Avoid legal actions by all-above-board dealings.

YOUR PET
A toy-grabber. The dog that snatches the biggest bone. The cat with the cream. Greedy.

The 3rd House
YOU
Brilliant ideas. Secret meetings to discuss plots. The super-spy 007. Fixed thoughts on certain subjects. Mysterious encounters. Important documents. Beware of revolutions.

YOUR PET
Leads all the rest on crazy ventures. Pinches the supper. Really smart.

The 4th House
YOU
There are often arguments at home. You'd like to be in charge of your own house, and will enjoy living close to nature. In fact, you would live in a cave or, even better, a tent. You'll tour the world.

YOUR PET
Happiest in the woods or playing on grass. Loves very long walks. Likes nuts and fruit.

The 5th House
YOU
You have a strong personality. Happiness is yours through creative work. Love partners fall under your spell. Beware of being too popular with the opposite sex. Inspired in art.

YOUR PET
Popular, likes to be with other animals. Happiest with same breed, opposite sex.

The 6th House
YOU
Working in a caring profession, healing others, is well aspected. There are psychic influences. You're quite diet-conscious. You'll make rapid improvements through personal efforts.

YOUR PET
Sometimes difficult to teach, then really clever. Nice when it wants to be, but changes quickly.

The 7th House
YOU
Great changes come through friends and lovers. You need to understand the feelings of others. Admired by that special one in your life. Many friends with mystical psychic powers.

YOUR PET
Likes to share your every minute. Your best pal. This pet looks to you for love.

The 8th House
YOU
Better to work alone. You have the power to develop moneymaking projects. You may make money by use of your psychic powers, astrology, or something similar. Do not abuse your gifts.

YOUR PET
Very sensitive and tuned in to you. Knows when you are happy or sad.

The 9th House
YOU
Pure-minded and very upright. Others look to you for moral guidance. Likely to become highly qualified and well educated. May be active in a religious movement, even as a spiritual leader.

YOUR PET
A goody-goody pet that will do no wrong. Great guard Very proud of itself and you

The 10th House
YOU
You will succeed. Others seek your advice on future prospects, and you have a reputation for being right. Outspoken, you make many friends and just as many enemies. Ambitious. Religious.

YOUR PET
Good-looking and admired by others. Wins prizes in cat or dog shows.

The 11th House
YOU
Influential friends will help you. Working with others brings benefits if you are fair and true, otherwise big trouble. A team leader. You may join weird societies and have strange friends.

YOUR PET
The pet that everybody wants to cuddle. May have odd friends calling round, stray cats or nosy squirrels.

The 12th House
YOU
With your telepathic powers and psychic gifts, you will sense when things are right or wrong. Never dabble with magic or the occult. Meditation brings peace. Seek truth through study.

YOUR PET
Mind-reading psychic pet that seems to know your thoughts. Given to staring at the Moon.

ASTRO-DOWSING

This is a totally new and unique way for you to read your own and your pet's characters. By using the astro-dowsing technique, you will be able to cast horoscopes for yourself and your pet. Then refer to the sections on the planets and the twelve houses to see what it all means.

EXPLANATION

Q: What is dowsing?
A: It is a way to find objects or the answers to questions by the use of such implements as sticks, rods, or a pendulum.
Q: How can this work?
A: We don't know. Some people think that there is a field of energy surrounding each one of us that has an effect on the dowsing instrument. Others believe that the instrument is tuned in to the energies of the Earth or even the universe. The pendulum will swing to and fro or move in a circle when it locates the object or answer sought.
Q: Who discovered or invented dowsing?
A: Dowsing existed before humankind began keeping records. The first known reference to dowsing is to be found deep in the Sahara desert at the Tassili-n-Ajjer caves where, over 8,000 years ago, someone drew a picture of people dowsing with Y-shaped rods.

The Bible tells the story of Moses finding water using his rod. The mythological ancient Greek inventor Daedalus has been credited with making the first pendulum.
Q: What is astro-dowsing?
A: It is an original method of creating a horoscope by using a pendulum to dowse the Astro-Dowsing Chart created by the author. You ask the questions listed, then complete a very simple form (page 90), putting in the answers you receive from the pendulum.
Q: Can I test this to see if it works?
A: Yes, go to the Astro-Dowsing Chart, or make your own copy and follow this simple one-question programme.

1) Hold the thread of the pendulum so that the tip of the crystal (or whatever you are using as a pendulum) is suspended over the centre of the Astro-Dowsing Chart. The pendulum must have enough thread to swing freely.

2) In your mind, picture your star sign. Concentrate on this for at least a full minute. Say the name of your star sign out loud: "Leo" or "Virgo" or whatever it is.

3) Now ask the pendulum to go to your star sign. Say out loud "What is my star sign?" in a clear and commanding voice.

4) Allow the pendulum to move of its own accord. Don't try to swing it. Watch as it moves toward your sign. Gently move the hand holding it in the direction of its pull. When you are directly over the symbol for your star sign, the pendulum should be swinging.

5) A further test is to ask one of your friends to sit beside you. Get them to tell you the name of their mother or father. Picture this person in your mind and speak their name out loud for at least one full minute.

6) Repeat the action as in 3 and 4 above. Say: "Tell me the star sign of my friends mother/father, Mrs/Mr XYZ." Watch as the pendulum swings and allow it to move freely. Once again, when it is over the correct star-sign symbol, it will swing in such a way that you will know it has selected the answer. Then ask your friend whether this is correct. You will be amazed to discover that indeed it is. You have now proved to yourself that astro-dowsing actually works.

Q: What next?

A: Astro-dowse your own chart using the method described below. Then refer to the sections on the houses and the planets to interpret your chart. Prepare to be astounded.

ASTRO-DOWSING INSTRUCTIONS

1) Place your Astro-Dowsing Chart so the top is facing south and the bottom is facing north.

2) Hold a pendulum over the center of the chart and ask it out loud to go to your star sign. When it does so correctly, you have tuned in to the universe.

3) With peace and love in your mind, ask the pendulum the following ten questions:

Q 1. In which of my 12 houses is the Sun?
Q 2. In which of my 12 houses is the Moon?
Q 3. In which of my 12 houses is Jupiter?
Q 4. In which of my 12 houses is Uranus?
Q 5. In which of my 12 houses is Mercury?
Q 6. In which of my 12 houses is Venus?
Q 7. In which of my 12 houses is Neptune?
Q 8. In which of my 12 houses is Saturn?
Q 9. In which of my 12 houses is Mars?
Q 10. In which of my 12 houses is Pluto?

Hold the tip of the pendulum over the planet symbol. Speak these questions out loud and picture the planet symbol in your mind. You should lead the pendulum round the chart through the twelve houses in an anti-clockwise motion, beginning in the 1st house. The pendulum will swing when it is held over the house it wants the planet in. When the pendulum swings, simply note the house and write the name of the planet on the form below.

Note that it is possible to have two or even more planets in a house. Just leave it up to the pendulum.

4) There is also a form for your pet, so when you have completed yours, do your pet's.

5) Consult the section explaining the power of the planets in the houses (page 71) to discover the meaning of your own or your pet's chart as obtained by astro-dowsing. Write into your personal astro-dowsing form the meanings given. For example, if you have the Sun in your 1st house, you would copy down the character assessment given, which is "Great power to lead others. Strong willpower. Imaginative and creative. Clear thinking. Determined and forceful. Energetic and very active. Healthy and strong. Ambitious. Brave."

MY ASTRO-DOWSING FORM
THE 12 HOUSES

NAME:..
Date of Birth..

STAR SIGN...

The 1st House:
PLANET/PLANETS:...
MEANING:...
....

The 2nd House:
PLANET/PLANETS:...
MEANING:...
....

The 3rd House:
PLANET/PLANETS:...
MEANING:...
....

The 4th House:
PLANET/PLANETS:...
MEANING:...
....

The 5th House:
PLANET/PLANETS:...
MEANING:...
....

The 6th House:
PLANET/PLANETS:...
MEANING:...
....

The 7th House:
PLANET/PLANETS:...
MEANING:...
....

The 8th House:
PLANET/PLANETS:...
MEANING:...
....

The 9th House:
PLANET/PLANETS:...
MEANING:...
....

The 10th House:
PLANET/PLANETS:...

MEANING:...
....

The 11th House:
PLANET/PLANETS:...
MEANING:...
....

The 12th House:
PLANET/PLANETS:...
MEANING:...
....

MY PET'S ASTRO-DOWSING FORM

THE 12 HOUSES
NAME:...
Date of Birth..
STAR SIGN..

The 1st House:
PLANET/PLANETS:...
MEANING:...
....

The 2nd House:
PLANET/PLANETS:...
MEANING:...
....

The 3rd House:
PLANET/PLANETS:...
MEANING:...
....

The 4th House:
PLANET/PLANETS:...
MEANING:...
....

The 5th House:
PLANET/PLANETS:...
MEANING:...
....

The 6th House:
PLANET/PLANETS:..
MEANING:...
....

The 7th House:
PLANET/PLANETS:..
MEANING:...
....

The 8th House:
PLANET/PLANETS:..
MEANING:...
....

The 9th House:
PLANET/PLANETS:..
MEANING:...
....

The 10th House:
PLANET/PLANETS:..
MEANING:...
....

The 11th House:
PLANET/PLANETS:..
MEANING:...
....

The 12th House:
PLANET/PLANETS:..
MEANING:...
....

YOUR PET'S LUCKY PLANET-POWER PENDANT

Each of the twelve star signs is ruled by a planet or planets. We have explained which planets rule which star signs. Now you can bring your knowledge together and create a lucky planet-power pendant for your pet's collar.

All you have to do is identify your pet's star sign and follow these simple instructions:
1) Across you will see the names of each of the twelve star signs with their symbols. Simply select the right one for your pet and copy it carefully.
2) Across you will see the names of each of the ten planets with their symbols. Simply select the right one for your pet and copy it carefully.
3) Insert into a pendant or make one yourself.
a) Place the star-sign name and symbol inside.
b) Place the planet name and symbol inside.
4) Now close the pendant firmly and attach this to your pet's collar.
5) Once the planet-power pendant has been fitted firmly into place, stroke your pet's head and say: "May this bring you lots of good luck!"
6) Your pet is now wearing the lucky planet-power pendant and should enjoy a happy and contented life.
Remember, you alone can make your pet's life fun. The power of the pendant will help you to do this.

 PISCES

 TAURUS

 CANCER

 AQUARIUS

 ARIES

 GEMINI

 VIRGO

 SCORPIO

 CAPRICORN

 LEO

 LIBRA

 SAGITTARIUS

 NEPTUNE   JUPITER   PLUTO   THE MOON   THE SUN

SATURN   MERCURY   MARS   URANUS   VENUS